Heavy Metal

My Story of Gui...., ...gnts,
Heavy Metal Workout
Albums, Passion, and Building
Muscle

Jason Stallworth

Dedicated to my cousin Kelly Stallworth
9/11/1973 - 9/23/2007

THANK YOU

Mom and Dad for always believing in me,
and to my soul mate, Candy for your constant love and support,
encouraging me to follow my dreams

"Weight" of the World

'Dhuun Dun-Dun-Dun, Duna-Dun-Dun, Dun-Dun-Dun, Duna-Dun-Dun, Dun-Dun-Dun, Duna-Dun-Dun, Dun-Dun Dhuun-Dun-Dun.'

- 'Weight of the World' - Heavy Metal Workout

I remember standing there daydreaming in the middle of the field during football practice. I was about eleven years old or so. My brain was more than likely pondering cartoons, G.I. Joes, Transformers, or some fantasy role playing game. Oddly enough, I never played Dungeons & Dragons, although I was fascinated by that whole concept. I did play some other RPGs. For those in the dark on this acronym, it stands for Role Playing Games.

Anyway, so I'm standing there off in my own little la-la land, and suddenly…*smack*! I got clocked, man! Both feet came off the ground and I found myself flying through the air in slow motion, and finally landed flat on my back. Some dude twice my size nailed me. I'm not sure if he did it on purpose to teach me a lesson, or to weed out the ones that really didn't belong there. It was extremely obvious I did not belong in that camp. I think he felt a little self-reproach afterwards, as he reached out his hand and helped me up. I certainly wasn't a threat to his position as my position was bench warmer, and rightfully so.

Dad (which I'll state up front that I could not have asked for better parents) wanted me to play sports, and I guess a part of me did too. Maybe I thought it just sounded cool telling people "Yeah, I play football and stuff!"

The truth is, I was terrified of playing team sports and easily intimidated. I downright sucked at sports except for backyard ball, and with that, I was only "pretend" good. Another truth is that I always looked at others as better than me when it came to sports or any competitive activities. For the most part, they were.

You see, I was a small, skinny kid growing up in a little town outside of Pensacola, Florida called Cantonment. We were really between Cantonment and Molino. Yes, I realize you've never heard of these places. They do indeed exist on Google Maps. I wasn't a complete runt, but I certainly didn't fit into the class of athletes and jocks, or the so-called elites of any sort.

I got picked on quite a bit. No, I'm not going to make this some sob story like a country song where I lost everything. I will say there's one thing about being the smaller kid that gets picked on: you feel completely powerless. Back then, the term "bullying" didn't exist as we know it today. You either fought back or just took it. Being non-aggressive by nature, I just took it.

As I recall several unfortunate incidents growing up, there's one that sticks out. There was this really big kid in middle school (he was possibly a grade or two behind). He would choose random people in class to pick on. I tried so hard to look away and keep to myself, kind of like pulling the sheets over your head so the ghosts can't see you. One day I was lucky enough to win the lottery ticket of turmoil. He looked over at me and said, "What the f&*k are you looking at?"

I found this to be strange since I was trying so hard to avoid him, but these kinds of people sense fear like some wild animal. Of course, I mumbled that I wasn't looking at anything, and I'm sure my voice was crackling because I was seriously scared. He proceeded with "Yeah, you better be scared of me 'cause I'll beat your ass!"

It gets better, and this is the part that's so vividly lodged in my memory. The next day I was walking down the hall on the way to class or something. That same kid came out of nowhere and slammed me against the lockers and told me he was going beat my ass. I'm guessing he rehearsed his lines as this is what he told me the day prior.

I was helpless and I'll admit that I was freaked out at this point. It didn't help that this cute girl I liked saw the whole thing go down. For whatever reason, I don't recall seeing him again, not in that context anyway. That was when this thing inside started brewing. I wanted to be big. Not so I could be a jerk like this guy, but so no one would mess with me. I could possibly be the backup to others that couldn't fend for themselves when confronted by these senseless ignoramuses. I remember the Three Stooges using this word and I always thought it was hilarious…ignoramus! I wanted to be a superhero, and I wanted cartoon-looking muscles!

Of course, that all changed when I turned 19. I had been drinking milk! Lol…I'm totally kidding. I stole that from the old 80's TV commercial! Remember that line, "And this is how I'm going to look when I'm 19! I don't forget a name, or a face!"

Okay, back to the real story…

Middle school was no fun. High school wasn't either, but middle school was, in fact, horrible. Physically, I was a bit behind. There was a little gym at our school and I would go in there and mess around with the machines when no one was in there. It's funny because no one really worked out. It was more like guys just trying to see who could lift the most. I was truly interested in lifting weights. I just didn't know anything about them and was too embarrassed at that time to ask or try.

I was about 14 years old when I picked up my first weight. My dad got me some of those old cement-filled plastic weights. Remember those? We had the long bar, two short bars for dumbbells, and a bench out in the back yard by our shed. The equipment was a bit worn and rusted. I believe we got it used at a yard sale or something. It had that rugged feel to it, which I liked. It seemed a little more hardcore, not that I was hardcore. I totally wasn't, but the concept fit the notion of me going into barbarian mode, based on some comics and games I had. Plus, working out in the elements made it that much tougher. Florida humidity is brutal. Perhaps there was a tiny bit of stoicism in me after all.

My parents encouraged me to lift weights, and my uncle Frankie (one of my mom's brothers) started coming over to lift with me as well. I had no clue what I was doing, but they showed me the basic exercises. I remember doing bench press, military press, and curls. I always thought military press was cool because I was a G.I. Joe fanatic.

I don't think we had an actual workout schedule. We just trained a few times per week. I wasn't strong, but I enjoyed lifting and always looked forward to it.

Looking back, it's amazing what you can do with the bare minimum. I didn't have a state of the art gym like you see on every corner these days. We had weights at school, but do you remember that part about me being easily intimidated? Yeah, that wasn't happening, so during my high school years, I stuck with what we had in the backyard at home. I learned new exercises, and little by little, made progress.

I was a huge (no pun intended) fan of Arnold Schwarzenegger. I shouldn't say *was*; I still am! I watched all his movies, and Stallone movies as well. I started reading the bodybuilding magazines. It was Joe Weider's *Muscle & Fitness*, and I believe *Flex* was around as well (I just Googled it; confirmed - the first issue of *Flex* was in 1983). I saturated myself in bodybuilding and strength training, learning all that I could absorb.

About a year into it, I started noticing changes. I was growing, but, by no means, was I big. Some people would sprout up the moment they looked at a weight. Not me, I was a true hard-gainer. And seriously, I ate food like someone was going to steal it from me. Muscle growth was extremely slow. Nonetheless, I stuck with it. I loved the way it made me feel (that was very close to a Michael Jackson pun, *The Way You Make Me Feel*).

Throughout high school I made incremental gains. Some of my friends noticed, which felt good. I kept reading the bodybuilding magazines and listening to advice of those more advanced.

I got ahead of myself at one point during my senior year and tried out for the football team. That didn't work out so well. The coaches placed me with the junior varsity team and most of those guys were stronger and faster than me. That was a huge wake-up call. Sports, or anything competitive, was never really my thing anyway. I had to take a step back and ask myself why I was doing what I was doing: To impress someone? Prove myself?

Despite whatever the reason was, I ended up walking off the practice field one day. It was after this kid tried to knock me down because I had performed one of the training drills wrong. As a result, the coach made the whole team suffer for my mistake by extending the running distance of the drill. They were all pretty pissed at me. I'll blame this on daydreaming again.

As discouraging as that time was, I didn't let it shake my love for the weights. Like Joe Dirt once said, "You gotta keep on keeping on."

Fast-forward a few years and I had finally started putting on what I considered to be real muscle mass. I broke the 200-pound mark in my mid-20's and was still in decent conditioning with definition and striations.

I never dove fully into bodybuilding in terms of competing or anything like that, but I was consistent with training and kept up with the sport (Yes, I consider bodybuilding a sport). I was never naturally strong, so I figured powerlifting wasn't in the cards for me. Oddly enough, as I write this, I'm starting to cater my workouts to more of a strength training style focusing on compound lifts and heavy weights.

Although I did get stronger over the years, I was more in tune with the physique transformation effects. In other words, I cared more about looking big than being strong; more show than go. If I had it to do over again knowing what I know now, I would have certainly focused more on strength. However, as the Metallica lyrics go, "No remorse, no regrets!"

As I progressed, I started training in the early mornings to avoid the evening gym crowd and that's been a schedule that I've adhered to throughout my life. That crowd is indeed a unique and special one. For someone to wake up at 4:30AM and be on their first set by 5:00AM, they're serious about what they're doing whether it's at a competitive level or just for the mere sake of their health. I've met a lot of really cool people in those early morning gym sessions from all walks of life.

I never had any plans to become a bodybuilder or powerlifter. It was just something I really enjoyed. This is one of those things that becomes a part of who you are. Even in my younger adult years, I knew I would continue lifting for the rest of my life. A lot of people will work out during high school or college, especially if they're playing sports, but once they become adults, they drop it. Then they find every excuse in the world as to why they don't workout consistently anymore. "I don't have time" is the most common line. Even though I had no aspirations to be a pro of any sort, it was much deeper than that for me. You could even call it a spiritual experience. The gym is my church.

Though growth was a slow process in my early years, I stuck with it and never once have I strayed from it. Lifting weights ultimately helped me build confidence and I truly believe the successes I've had in life are attributed to where it all started; pumping out reps with those cement-filled weights in the back yard.

Captivated by Power Chords

'Hello me, meet the real me.'

- Dave Mustaine

Some people start out of the gate being gifted. I didn't think anything was in the cards for me in that regard. Sure, I was lifting weights semi-consistently and loving it, but there was something else brewing deep inside. I just had no clue what it was at that time.

We all search. Oftentimes we're lost and not quite sure what we're searching for, but we know it's something that's burning in our soul. And one day it sort of "hit me like a two-ton heavy thing". Yes, that was from Queensryche. Can you name the song and album without looking it up?

It was like I had stumbled upon this secret portal to another dimension. Narnia is the first thing that comes to mind. I discovered the guitar soon after stumbling upon heavy metal music.

Before I talk about how I got into music, let's back up a little. There's an interesting story that leads into all of this, and it all sort of comes together.

Prior to getting into weightlifting, I had been riding bikes for several years. My friends and I were heavily into BMX freestyle. Remember the movie *Rad* from the 80s? That's what we wanted to be, and we were in our own way. I'd lift weights when I got home from school and then hop on my bike.

I guess you could say that I grew up out in the country. There were only a few houses on our street. It wasn't a big suburban neighborhood like what you see in *The Goonies*. I'm only reminded of *The Goonies* because of the many daring adventures of my own childhood, though we weren't chased by bad guys or anything. We were chased a few times, but I don't think they wanted to kill us! Anyway, there was a dirt road that connected to our street. That led into the woods with many trails, a huge clay pit, and a creek called Cow Devil's Creek (that would be a cool name for a metal band).

Being kings of our neighborhood, we rode our bikes all over the place, exploring the trails and anywhere we could get our bikes through. We would discover new dirt roads and ultimately end up in other parts of town. Our area was a safe place, except for the bike ramps we built which resulted in many busts! I'm very thankful for an active and outdoors childhood.

We probably would have been better off with mountain bikes with all our voyages and quests, but those didn't look cool to me. What looked cool was BMX freestyle bikes, so I had an older model. I got into doing tricks, and soon freestyling became an everyday event.

My parents bought me my first real freestyle bike the Christmas of 1990. It was a GT Pro Performer. Shocks, pegs; lucky! It had everything and was chromed out like Destro! Now, even though I had stopped believing in Santa at that age, my mom and dad would still wake up in the middle of the night and put the presents under the tree in the living room like Santa dropped them off. We also had a chimney, so the scene was complete. I would even leave out cookies and milk.

Sometimes in life it's not necessarily whether something is real, it's simply the enjoyment of the act and living in that moment of fantasy. I remember waking up super early as usual and seeing my new freestyle bike. Talk about being stoked! I said stoked, not spoked so not quite a pun there. Actually, my bike didn't have spokes, it had mags!

Music and riding BMX bikes was a cool and obvious mix. They just naturally fit. I had a Sony Walkman. That was the coolest device ever for listening to music with headphones. I'd ride for hours just listening to tunes. There was a complete sense of freedom that came with that.

I found myself gravitating towards harder music. Although back then you never heard heavy metal on the radio. About the heaviest music on the radio were hair bands and hard rock bands like Bon Jovi, Poison, Whitesnake, Scorpions, Warrant, etc.

I'll never forget the day I heard a very specific sound that I'd never heard before. It spoke to me like a voice from the Heavens and punched me right in my soul.

There was this kid on the bus that had his headphones on going spastic playing air drums. I didn't really know this dude, and he was a hit or miss as far as going to school was concerned. I had this admiration for him right away. He had long hair and wore a jean jacket covered in sew-on patches with the names of metal bands all over it. The music was blaring, and he was going crazy!

Other kids on the bus were making fun of him, calling him a weirdo and such, and asking him how he could listen to that devil music. No one messed with him because he was an extreme non-conformist, and carried that with a sense of pride. They were probably a little afraid of him. Metal music back then had an immediate stereotype of being Satanic, but to me, he was the coolest dude on the bus.

I could hear these clanging, chunky sounds coming from his headphones. I had to know what this was, so I built up the courage and asked "Man, that sounds cool, what band are you listening to?"

He removed one ear piece. With a grin, as if he were ecstatic at the potential to create a fan of this underground genre that most people discarded as noise, said "Metallica!".

He then went back to his air drumming. If I recall, it was the Justice album.

I ended up hanging out with this dude later and listening to him play guitar. He had a record player and many albums from Metallica, Megadeth, Slayer, Iron Maiden, and so forth.

That weekend, I had someone drive me to the store, and with my savings from mowing lawns, I bought my first two heavy metal albums. Metallica's *Master of Puppets* and *And Justice for All*.

I immediately became obsessed. These albums ran in my tape player non-stop. They powered me through both my workouts and freestyling bikes. From there, I ventured deeper into the world of metal music with bands like Megadeth, Slayer, etc. It was like being reborn.

Before I get into the meat and potatoes of how I started playing guitar, let me back up several years to my early childhood. I was mesmerized by music and was recording songs off the radio at the age of eight (we had these ancient devices called tapes). Back in those days, the radio hits were artists like Prince, Madonna, Phil Collins, The Police, I could go on for days here. I also remember how it would tick me off when the DJ would still be talking during the intro to a song I liked. I was like, "Dude, shut up!"

So the love for music in general had been there from early on.

Now, back to metal!

I loved metal music, but there was still something missing. I wanted more. In other words, I didn't want to just listen to it. I wanted to be a part of it.

Something magical happened when I heard that first power chord. I had this yearning to create the music I was hearing. I found my true passion and knew exactly what I wanted to do with my life. I just didn't quite know where to start.

My Uncle Freddie (my dad's brother) had this old acoustic guitar sitting in the closet. It had four rusty strings on it. I picked it up and started messing around with it. By ear, I learned the basic notes for *Iron Man* from Black Sabbath, as if I have to tell you the name of the band. From there, I started picking out more songs I heard, but just playing the melodies with single-note riffs. I didn't know anything about chords or scales, but the whole process felt natural.

When I say it "felt natural", it doesn't mean that I started playing Malmsteen-style sweep arpeggios right away. I did learn quite fast and playing guitar felt like something that I was meant to do. This was a huge relief to find something that fit. Sure, I enjoyed lifting weights and BMX, but I could never seem to get past a certain point with either of those no matter how hard I tried or how much I practiced. Playing guitar was a completely different story. I experienced several moments of early success in my playing.

My dad and uncle saw that I was getting serious with it ("I'd say things are getting pretty serious" - Kip from Napoleon Dynamite, in case you didn't catch that). So they bought some new strings, showed me how to string it up, and also picked up a Mel Bay chord book. I learned the basic chords and continued learning rock and metal songs.

I wasn't much for textbook learning. The only classes I did well in were English and Creative Writing. I think music theory is

18

great for most musicians, and it's important to learn. I associated that type of learning to being in school, and I didn't want guitar playing to feel like that. I found from day one that I was good at picking things out by ear. I never even learned beyond the basic major/minor scales. Rather, I made up my own practice patterns, which in essence, were scales that I was unaware of at the time. I'm not telling you this to deter you from learning theory. This is simply part of my history of how I got started.

Soon after, Dad saw that I clearly wanted to take it to the next level. He reached out to his friend, who was and still is a well-known local musician in Pensacola, to help pick out a starter electric guitar and amp for me. It was a bright red Gremlin guitar and small Dean Markley amp. I had a choice to get a used Ibanez for the same price as the Gremlin, and should've went with that, but I didn't know any better. Besides, red is the color of blood and that seemed more metal-looking than the used Ibanez that was available. Everything was perfect for the time.

I do feel kind of bad because my parents had just spent a decent amount of money on my GT Pro Performer freestyle bike. Here we were a month or so after Christmas buying a guitar and amp. God bless them! I guess I was somewhat high maintenance, but I think they sensed that this was something deeper than a mere hobby that I would pick for a while only to get bored with six months later. I think they knew this was more along the lines of a calling.

As far as textbook learning is concerned, I never went too much further beyond the basics. I wanted to learn how to play Metallica and all the other bands I was listening to. I didn't think that theory would help me, though again, I'm not discouraging learning music theory. So that's what I did. I spent hours in my room learning songs and riffs. Eventually, I started making up my own riffs based on what I was learning.

I was playing some semi-complex guitar solos within my first year of picking up guitar. Soon after, I was known for speed. Fast guitar solos were my forte, so to speak. The funny thing is, I didn't learn how to alternate pick right away (this is picking back and forth...no, not picking your nose! Guitar!). I used all down-strokes (*huh, huh...I said stroke*).

I played in my church during my teenage years. Hey, Metal Church! Another band I listened to quite a bit, and yes, another pun. I told you there'd be more!

All jokes aside, some may say that learning heavy metal music and church music just don't mix or even the concepts of those two genres. I disagree. On the contrary, playing in church was great for me and expanded my abilities. Most of the church songs were old hymns in non-guitar-friendly keys and progressions. So, I was playing in weird keys like E flat, B flat and such instead of just E minor like with most metal and rock music.

My friend Alex, another accomplished guitar player, and I would switch leads in church. We had a blast! I must mention our mentor, Ronnie Goodman, a phenomenal musician and songwriter. He led the music and continuously encouraged us and helped us expand our talents. He was more of a jazz and blues player, but he would rip it up and down the fret board. He just did some amazing things with his instrument. That was a time I'll always be grateful for.

We formed a little band within the church and called ourselves Revelation. It was more of just us jamming, but playing in any capacity with other musicians adds to your experience and helps you further develop as a musician.

I joined my first of what I considered to be a real band after I graduated high school. By real band I mean one that's playing gigs. From there, I played in a few other bands, including my own. Though none of my bands ever "made it", I eventually started writing and recording my own music as a solo artist. There's a ton of events intertwined throughout those years, but I'll save those details for another book. Yes, my decorated band mates Eddie and Tom, I will write about you guys in the next book. This isn't my official autobiography, but I'll write that at some point…Hosers! Lol.

So that's the story, or rather a snapshot, of how I got started playing guitar, and my new-found love for heavy metal music. I mentioned the feeling of being reborn but sitting here now, it feels like the music within me was there from the very beginning. You have that as well, and we'll get into that later because I'm going to help you dig it up.

Metal and Weights

'Metal and weights; a marriage meant to last.'

- Jason Stallworth

Everything changed upon hearing that first power chord. It was like I had found the Holy Grail or meaning for life. I had an immediate love for heavy metal music. A love that would last a lifetime (indeed a Firehouse pun).

When I started playing guitar, that fire inside was ignited even more, thus the journey of music creation began. I wasn't sure where this would lead and didn't have any plans other than at some point, I knew I would release my own music to the world. It's like one of those things where you know the destination, although uncertain of the details, but you have no map in front of you on how to get there. You just have to make it up as you go, and as the folks in Fleetwood Mac would say, I went my own way.

I spent most of my teenage years developing my newly found passion. It was like something that had been there all along. Playing guitar felt so natural. It wasn't like everything else where I had to read the book three times to get it, so to speak. Sure, there were challenges at different levels as I grew as a musician. No matter what level you are on, there will always be challenges if you plan to progress, but for the most part, guitar was almost effortless for me.

Though I practically locked myself in my room for hours at a time, I still stuck with my weight training. Like playing guitar and writing music, lifting weights was something that I knew would never get old to me. It's never been anything I had to think about or push myself to do. Even today, it's one of those things that if I don't do it, I might as well just stay in bed for the rest of the day. It's second nature.

When you're extremely passionate about something, it's embedded. It's a part of you. There's nothing you can do to escape it. You can run from it, as many of us often run from our calling at some point, but it's always going to be there for you (these five words I swear to you…okay, okay, enough already, right?).

Sometimes we go through things, or make stupid decisions that put us in undesirable circumstances, that pull us away from what we know we need to be actively pursuing. But it eventually comes back around, hopefully. Because I'll tell you this, if you've been given a gift, it's downright shameful and wasteful not to use it and share it with the world. Man, that was kind of deep!

You know, we all go through trends and phases. Like the mullet hairstyle, or tight-rolling your jeans (Yes, I did that). Many gave into those fads, but they faded away after about ten years (much of the '80s leaked into the early '90s; just couldn't let go), and people stopped doing them.

Although I will occasionally come across a mullet sighting, as rare as they are, I'm thrown back to the non-aggressive mullet I saw getting dog food the other day: business in the front, party in the back. This particular mullet carried a "mulletude" rating of about 7.5. Looks fierce, but nothing to be afraid of.

Back to my point. Things change. Trends come and go. People, places, jean-rolling, high-top Reeboks, music, the paradigm shifts.

Not everything comes and goes. There are some things in life that remain. In fact, some things become even more set in stone and unmovable. For us metal heads, it's our music.

Even throughout my adult years I've had people tell me that my music tastes would change as I got older. I guess they were right. They did shift some. I've gotten into heavier music over the past few years: Amon Amarth, In Flames, Sabaton, Arch Enemy, to name a few.

Seriously, it's like some people expect you to start listening to smooth jazz or something once you turn forty. Nothing against jazz or any style of music, but if you're a true metal head, it's ingrained in you. It's not going to ever change because it's not supposed to. If it does, then you must question whether you were ever a true metal music lover versus just going along with whatever seemed cool at that time. It's one thing to be open and listen to other styles of music. I've always done that, but a true metal head will never stop listening to metal, and metal will always be the preferred choice.

To go along with that, I've seen so many people that lifted weights when they were younger stop when they became adults. They got married, had kids, got a career…blah, blah. All those things are fine but none of those should be an excuse to neglect your health. The truth is the older you get the more you should exercise!

I've met so many people that lifted weights during high school or college that are now so far from where they once were, and completely out of shape. Part of the problem is you have to develop a love for the weights. I'll take a quote from Tai Lopez from his *The 67 Steps*, "You have to learn to love the grind."

If you've gotten away from working out and find yourself making a hundred excuses, then set your alarm for 4:45AM tomorrow morning and go hit the gym. That's what I do, and there's no better time. Seriously. Do it. Hey! **Do it**.

Metal and weights have always been a huge part of my life since I was introduced to both. It's not a trend, and it was never a mere phase. It's not something you grow out of, and I love both metal and weights today more than I ever have. On that note, don't ever let anyone tell you that you're too old for something, that you should act or dress a certain way, or pursue what society says is appropriate. If everyone did that, we would lack the many inventions, entertainment, creative outlets, etc. that we have today.

For example, I'm sure the folks who write the scripts for *Teen Titans* are around my age (hence all of the '80s innuendoes), and I'm sure someone told them they were too old to be focused on cartoons at some point and probably tried to talk them into getting a typical nine to five gig. I'm glad they didn't listen if that was the case because that's an awesome show! Yes, I occasionally watch cartoons.

Why metal and weights? Obviously, you can do one or the other. You can lift weights to country or rap music, I guess. Some people do. To me, heavy metal music is more appropriate for working out in general. There's an aggression with metal that you just don't get with other genres of music. There's something about your headphones blaring with heavy metal guitars chugging away. Of course, that's just my opinion. Heck, I've seen people in the gym that don't typically listen to metal bobbing their heads when Pantera comes on. "Re-spect, walk! What did you say?"

Have that cranked up as you're walking over to the squat rack and I can almost guarantee you'll go fifty pounds heavier than usual. With that said, I've always been able to lift heavier and workout longer while listening to metal music in the gym, and I don't really have a playlist. I'll either listen to a full album which usually lasts for a weight training workout, or I'll listen to a radio station on iTunes based on a band I like.

Here's a cool example of a way you can break it down, coupling a metal album with each workout:

- **Chest Day:** Metallica - *Master of Puppets*

- **Back Day:** Amon Amarth - *Deceiver of the Gods*

- **Leg Day:** Jason Stallworth - *Heavy Metal Workout II*

- **Shoulder Day**: Arch Enemy - *War Eternal*

- **Arm Day:** Sabaton - *Art of War*

Yes, I threw one of my own albums in there!

As you can see, my metal tastes range from classic heavy metal to a wide range of modern metal; mostly bands from European countries. You could use this model and pick a different album for each workout, and probably never run out of metal albums to listen to. There are endless choices and so many sub-genres of metal music.

I tend to listen to stations based on artists or a song. This is a great way to find new bands. The only downfall is you might be in the middle of a set when a song starts playing that you don't really care for. That can be distracting, but the good outweighs the bad. You can play around with different tactics like a radio station-based workout one time, a full album the next.

I talk quite a bit about lifting weights because that's how it all started for me, but in all reality, working out doesn't have to be associated with only weights. There's a wide array of exercises and exercise philosophies. The important thing is to stay active. We were not built to live a sedentary lifestyle, even though I'm typing this as I'm reclining on the sofa, I'm going to go practice martial arts kicks on my patio in a few minutes…or perhaps I'll eat a bowl of ice cream instead! Okay, okay…martial arts it is!

I have friends that don't care for lifting weights. Instead, they'd rather run or train for those obstacle races like Tough Mudder or Spartan Races. Some people just take long walks every day. Others do functional training, or training geared towards a specific sport. As my third grade teacher once told me, "different strokes for different folks".

I personally think lifting weights is one of the best forms of exercises you can do for longevity, but I'm no doctor or health expert. I only have my own experience to base that on, and these days I'm integrating a variety of training such as martial arts and Yoga. I also do a ton of stretching these days. I plan to also get into Tai Chi at some point and do a deeper study of Karate, Muay Thai, and Kung Fu. I've been fascinated by martial arts since I was a kid but never seriously got into it until recently.

The point I'm making here is simple. I want to encourage everyone to do something. Chances are by picking up this book you're already working out. If so, kudos to you. Keep it up! If you're not, or if you're struggling with consistency, there's no better time than today to make those changes. If you're reading this at night, I'll accept you starting tomorrow!

Regardless of where you are, keep reading because I'll be sharing some of my personal workouts and workout concepts that have helped me over the years. Before we get there, I want to dive into the reason this book was written: the making of my *Heavy Metal Workout* album series.

The Making of the Heavy Metal Workout Album Series

Heavy Metal Workout

'Sleep my friend and you will see that dream is my reality.'

- James Hetfield

Heavy Metal Workout was my second studio album released in February of 2016. It's a classic style instrumental metal album. I'd like to take you back to where it all begin with the original *HMW*, although I'm not a fan of acronyms, I'll often refer to *Heavy Metal Workout* as *HMW*.

I released my first studio album, *Apocalyptic Dreams*, in 2013. This is an instrumental metal/hard rock album. It's more on the melodic side with a classic metal foundation, and this first album was a huge milestone. It's was one of those things I always wanted to do, but for whatever reason, it took me until my late thirties to do it. Nonetheless, I was so excited about this and I started writing new material almost immediately after the release.

The plan was to put out a second instrumental metal album two years after *Apocalyptic Dreams* was released. The new music and riffs I was writing were heavier and more driving than anything I'd ever written. I kept going back and forth with album titles. I even thought of calling it *Apocalyptic Dreams II*. I freely admit that I can be a bit indecisive on these types of things.

One day it hit me. I listen to metal while I work out, and well, while I do everything, for the most part. I started thinking of all the people I knew that embraced the driving force of heavy metal music while in the gym. I was like "Hmmm…heavy metal and heavy weights!"

Within a few seconds of that thought, the name popped in my head.

You know by now how much I love puns. *Heavy Metal Workout* is indeed just that, but it also makes perfect sense. There's a ton of metal workout playlists out there on Spotify, iTunes, Amazon, etc., but there was no original music specifically for working out, so I went for it.

A strange thing happened when I decided to sit down and start the creation process for *HMW*. I already had a decent amount of material written and recorded. I assumed I would use, or at least re-record much of what I already had down, but I didn't. I ended up starting from scratch. It's kind of like this book. I've deleted my fair share of sentences, and in some cases paragraphs. It's just part of the creative arts process.

One of the reasons I didn't use the material I had already written was because I had a very specific vision for *HMW*. The first goal was to choose a range of BPM (beats per minute) for the entire album. Not that I wanted every song to have the exact same pace, but I did want a range because I was looking for consistency. I established this through my own research, asking people what their favorite metal songs were when working out, and my own intuition and preferences.

For working out, you want something driving and steady. I didn't want any tempo changes or breaks or slow parts. Another important aspect to me was that the music was melodic and kept you pumped. I also didn't want the music to be distracting. A huge help was the fact that this was going to be an instrumental album. This was also part of my research in asking what people preferred to listen to while working out.

I had extremely positive responses when asking if they would like to have some classic heavy metal style instrumental music for their workouts. Vocals and lyrics can sometimes be distracting. Have you ever heard metal music that you really liked but just couldn't get past the vocals? I like a wide variety of metal vocal styles, but they can be hit or miss. The focus of *HMW* was all about the music, and all about we gym rats. I wanted to ensure motivation, pump, focus, and energy kind of like a pre-workout supplement.

The same concept was followed for the guitar solos. Lead guitar has always been my forte but I knew I needed to hold back a little. There are some fast guitar solos in *HMW*, but I wanted to make sure the song flowed and, again, wasn't distracting.

With all that said, I also wanted a classic heavy metal feel to the album. When I say classic, I mean mid to late '80s and early '90s heavy metal style, not hair metal, although I was a pretty big fan of it back then...I guess I still am. I've been listening to a lot of Warrant, Whitesnake, Dokken, and a few others lately. I wanted more of an older Metallica, Judas Priest, and Megadeth style with a modern twist.

I wrote all of the rhythm parts for the first *HMW* album within about a month. You'd find me in the studio 2-3 evenings a week writing the guitar parts and I'd spend a block of several hours recording on the weekends.

Now, I can crank out new music fairly quickly, but I don't end up using it all. For example, I may write a song but only use a part of it. Sometimes I'll go back and listen and decide I don't care for it, and trash it altogether. Again, that's just part of the creative process. Whether it's music, writing a book or a screen play, drawing, painting, there may be parts you delete, so to speak, before the final draft.

Writing and recording *HMW* was a magical experience. The ideas and riffs just kept coming. It was almost like I wasn't writing and there was some magical invisible gnome, or maybe even a dragon (I like dragons) writing the music through me. I'm a huge fan of things that are effortless like pressing the button on the remote to go to the next Netflix series. Recording *HMW* wasn't quite that effortless. but I'm sure you get it. There's a natural flow that you get into when the universe is seemingly aligned in your favor.

A side note for you guitar players and musicians: I typically record as I write music. The modern-day recording process

32

allows you to easily do that. I'll record one initial guitar track. Once I touch it up, add/remove pieces and perfect it, I'll go back and re-record that track from start to finish. Then I'll record a second rhythm guitar track. My style is to record two rhythm tracks and hardpan each, which means you'll hear one guitar in the left speaker and the other in the right. This adds fullness to the overall mix and works great if you want to have harmonizing guitar parts.

Once I have the rhythm guitar tracks recorded, I lay the bass guitar tracks. After that, the drums. Drums are the one thing I do not play, or at least not well enough to keep up with the music that I write. I hire that part out to a professional drummer.

The last tracks I record are the lead guitar tracks, and this is usually the most time-consuming part of the whole process. I may do a hundred takes in some cases even for a short guitar solo. Other times I may like what I put down the first time. Being a lead guitarist, I'm very picky and hard on myself here.

However, with *HMW*, I didn't spend as much time on the leads. Again, the theme was based on captivating melodies over speed, though the album does have its fair share of shredding. I chose to do what I felt was best for each song and the overall album. Sometimes that can be a you against yourself struggle. That's a nice way of saying "ego".

Although we're talking specifically about the making of *Heavy Metal Workout*, I pretty much just told you my process for recording music in general. If that's an interest of yours, look up my YouTube channel - https://www.youtube.com/channel/UCY7K3zmRSS6ZiEdj09K HnpQ. I have a ton of guitar lessons and recording tip videos.

Heavy Metal Workout II

Once I released *HMW* in February 2016, I started recording new music with more aggressive rhythms. At the time, I had recently started listening to a lot of heavier bands like Amon Amarth, Kreator, Exodus, and Arch Enemy. All that stuff was coming out in my writing. It had a melodic death metal feel to it.

I must say this was the heaviest music I had ever written. I let a couple of my close and trusted musician friends hear some of clips of what I was writing. They were shocked and somewhat floored as they had never heard anything like this come out of me. Yeah, I've always played heavy music, but this was on another level of heavy.

It was almost like some sort of possession, or some force came over me during the writing process of what would ultimately become *Heavy Metal Workout II*. No, there are no subliminal messages other than you better get in the gym and train insane. *Train Insane* is actually a track from the first *HMW* album.

The creation of music and most all forms of art have their timelines, and it doesn't so much depend on when you want to put something out there. I still haven't figured out how this works. In theory, I'd just lock myself in my studio every night for a couple of hours. It seems to be only select times when the music releases itself from deep within your inner being, at least in my experience, and there are a ton of things that can get in the way.

There's the concept of life happening, and that could be your job, a business, family, or any of the many things that life throws our way (which isn't necessarily always a bad thing). There are also other elements that can get in your way in the studio. I'll talk more about this in a later chapter. To counter that, don't be lazy about pursuing your craft. For anything to happen, you have to be doing something, and that often means doing something even when you don't feel like it.

Getting back to the process of creating *HMW II*: if you're a musician, especially a guitar player, you understand the endless search for guitar tone. It seems you find the perfect tone, love it, record with it, but then the very next day you're searching for something better.

I wanted a different and darker sounding guitar tone for *HMW II*. I didn't want to use the same thing I used for the *HMW*. *HMW II* was far more aggressive and faster with a lot of death metal style riffs. I wanted a tone that would complement and fit the music.

I was consistent at writing the riffs, but I found myself in tone hell, going back and forth between amps. I would write a few songs and then I'd mess around with tones. Technology doesn't help with virtual amps (what's known as plug-ins) and amp modeling, you have endless tone capabilities. Where this might sound like a guitar player's dream come true, it's really a nightmare in which you can easily get lost and swept away from what you should be spending more time doing: writing and recording music.

I wrote and recorded most of the rhythm tracks within a short amount of time, maybe three months, give or take. Because the riffs were so fast, I found myself going back and doing more takes. Your music should always be tight, but the faster you play, the tighter it needs to be. Otherwise it's going to sound like crap. There's room for some organic nuances that you may keep because it sounds cool and almost impossible to recapture. Your timing and all of the instruments should be in sync. No dude, not the boy band 'NSync…seriously?

Though *HMW II* ended up being more of an instrumental death metal style album, I kept it melodic. I've never been a fan of mere noise or banging on all the instruments just to be loud. I want the notes and progressions to tell a story and sing out. This posed an even greater challenge. I wasn't just writing heavy metal or death metal music. I was writing yet another album for the workout music category. Like the first *HMW*, I didn't want this album to be distracting either. It had to flow. At the same time, you run the risk of all the songs sounding similar. This became a challenge from multiple angles.

Guitar solos were the first thing that came to mind. Sure, there needed to be some shredding and there is, but I didn't want it to be too off-the-wall or crazy. Just like vocals can be distracting while working out, so can solo parts of any sort. It's one of those things where the product is truly for a specific group of people. I had to balance creativity with fitting the music into this micro-niche. I had set rules and guidelines for myself. The music needed to fit my vision.

The toughest thing about following such a pattern is you can easily make yourself think that you're boxed in. It's like a producer telling the band they don't like this part and to change it, or like having a boss shoot down your idea and do what he or she thinks is best when you know their way is just downright boring or inefficient. Most of us have an extreme dislike for limitations, and we artists are all free spirits, so I had to keep reminding myself that this was my own idea.

I decided early on that I wasn't going to rush *HMW II*. I spent more time on recording the guitar and bass tracks, and of course the tones as well (ggrrrr!). I also decided I wasn't going to do the drum tracks myself. Whether using real drums or a program, I wanted the drum parts to be handled by an actual drummer. Not just any drummer, I wanted someone who had adequate experience and that had a solid reputation in the music industry. Luckily, I stumbled upon a local studio professional who's also an accomplished drummer and musician, Ed Aborn. When it was all said and done, the drum tracks turned out far better than anything I could've done on my own.

I mentioned how much time I spent on recording the guitars and bass tracks. Well, when I got the drum files back, I decided to re-record all the bass and some of the rhythm guitar tracks. I wanted to better match the bass lines with the new drum tracks. I recorded the original bass lines along with the drum loops I threw in there. It was good, but not great, and some of the rhythm guitars were clearly off in certain parts on two or three songs.

Now, I'm pretty good at not being overly anal or a perfectionist (huh, huh…I said anal…huh, huh). I'm more of a "just wing it" kind of guy and I've adopted the philosophy of "sometimes good enough is perfect". I say that because it's easy to screw something up by continuously trying to perfect it. When it comes to your own creation, something you're putting out there for the world to see and hear, you tend to look under every rock.

I can't tell you how many times I listened to those tracks. As I would listen, I would document things I didn't like or felt needed to be polished up. You have to find that balance and at some point, you just have to go with it and put it out there. If you don't, you'll continue the never-ending quest of finding imperfections and your product will never get released.

The writing and recording process for *HMW II* was a divine and cult-like experience all in one. I know that sounds crazy, but it consumed me, especially the initial writing process. I lived and breathed it for several months, and I was obsessed at the fact that this was the heaviest music I had ever written. I was like "Where has this music been all my life?"

As a musician and recording artist, I'm extremely happy with both *Heavy Metal Workout* albums. Though they're both instrumental metal, they're completely different in terms of style and aggression. My hope was to provide a dynamic volume of metal music: classic metal with a modern twist to melodic death metal. So, there you have it: instrumental heavy metal workout music.

The Ultimate Life Goal: Discovery and Pursuit of Passion

'The worst thing I can be is the same as everybody else. I hate that.'

- Arnold Schwarzenegger

We've been talking a bit about my experience of how I got started in what ultimately became two passions in my life. I've shared some behind the scenes and the making of the *Heavy Metal Workout* albums, and the overall concept. But this chapter and the next several chapters are going to be focused on you.

You may play guitar, and you may not. You may play drums or bass or keyboards, or maybe you sing. Maybe you paint or draw, or you have a knack for graphic arts. You may write novels, poetry, or screenplays. You may be an actor, or an aspiring actor venturing into the performing arts arena. You may be into fitness or bodybuilding, or some sort of physique transformation, which is an art of its own. You may be into strength training or powerlifting. You may be into martial arts, which is indeed an art. I recently got into martial arts and it's kicking my rear!

I could keep going, but the point I'm trying to make is there are so many passion-filled arts and activities to pursue. You may be in the boat with many people I've spoken to that feel like they don't have a creative side. Sure, these talents and gifts may come more natural to some than others, but by no means does that count you out.

Every one of us has something that drives us. It may not be obvious to you, and sometimes it takes just getting out there and trying new things to discover your passion. It's kind of like the writing process I talked about earlier. Often, the songs just don't randomly appear to me. I have to get in the studio and start playing. Only then does the magic start to happen.

I'll speak to those that may be in the older crowd. I'm in my early 40s. It's easy to think that it's too late for us to pursue or learn something new, and it may seem unrealistic to think that we can get great at something as we age. Sometimes it's something we used to be great at but we left behind because the dream just didn't fit the picture of life that society paints for us.

My generation was taught to do well in school, go to college, get a good job with benefits, save a little, and perhaps one day, retire. Most passion-driven gigs go against that grain, so we settled for a normal nine to five job to pay the bills. Anything outside of that was a mere fantasy and deemed as unrealistic. I don't know that it's much different today.

I remember the line from Stallone in Rocky Balboa that felt like a punch in the gut. At this point, Rocky had lived out his dreams defeating great fighters, winning championships, and accumulating wealth. Yes, I know, he lost it all later…well,

41

Paulie lost it all. Rocky's wife had recently passed away, and he was running his Italian restaurant leading a quiet life.

Rocky had subconsciously settled into a life that was far from the daily grind of intense training for a specific goal, and the excitement of stepping into the ring. Now, there's nothing wrong with settling down, but he was just kind of floating through life. However, he wasn't done, and if you're still breathing and reading this, neither are you.

We do that. Sometimes we just feel like we merely exist, and that there's nothing more that we can do with our lives. In a sense, we give up.

But then Rocky unleashes in tears. He says something to the effect of there being this thing, this beast inside, and he ultimately says "There's still some stuff in the basement."

That was powerful and moving. Heck, I'll admit, I shed a little tear during the movie. I think a lot of us that are past our so-called prime feel that way. Just coasting along, accepting the norm of society, but we know deep down there's that thing, that beast. It's looking for a fight, and something to train for.

I think younger folks can feel this way too. Maybe when you get out of high school, or graduate college, you may feel like you've lived your prime. One part of you is excited to be done and move on to the next phase in life, but there's another side that fears uncertainty.

What is it really going to be like? Are you going to end up in some job you hate, being financially trapped in it by a house and car payment, and settle into a mediocre life? You may feel you're beyond the highlights of your life.

The lyrics from John Mellencamp immediately come to mind: "Oh Yeah, life goes on, long after the thrill of living is gone."

That's a catchy tune and riff, but wow, that's depressing. It's almost like what's the point? What are we supposed to do? Just exist as part of a functioning unit of our home or society, like a lifeless machine?

I don't think so at all. And that's what this passage of words is all about. You may have had some highlights in your prior years. You may feel like you'll never recapture that. You won't. Trust me, but that doesn't mean you're dead, and it doesn't mean you can't create even greater moments and more monumental highlights in your life.

I'll never forget 2013. So many awesome things happened. My wife and I bought our first home together. Two days before we moved, Frodo was bestowed upon us. Frodo is our piebald Dachshund that we rescued off the street; indeed, a gracious and loving twist of fate. I got a decent promotion that year. I also bought my first brand new car. I had always driven beaters and was fed up with wondering if my car would crank or the AC would work, so I got a good deal on a Nissan Rogue. My wife later bought me some cool Metallica and Megadeth stickers to put on the back window. That purchase was much needed because my other car completely crapped out right after we moved into our home. Fortunately, a close family friend let us use one of her vehicles in the interim, which was another great thing for that year.

Lastly, to top it off, I released my first studio album in December of 2013, *Apocalyptic Dreams*. So yeah, it's tough to trump that year. You ride the high for a while, and in those moments, it feels like you're a part of that Van Halen song *Standing on Top of the World.*

I carried that momentum for a while but like most things in life, you find yourself back at square one at some point. It's like, okay, all that cool stuff happened a year ago, or two years…five, ten years ago. You start to think that was it. That was your best year and you may never experience anything like that again.

I know I said this chapter was about you and not about me; I'm sharing this in hopes that you can relate. I think most of you can. It's easy to fall into that mind trap that tells us the "good ole days" are behind us. Now we just have to exist from here on out, and hope for the best. I think I'd rather try my luck blowing my paycheck at the casino or something! I'm halfway joking; I only take a twenty-dollar bill for the slot machines. Well, sometimes two twenty-dollar bills.

We go through peaks and valleys in life, and oftentimes it seems there are far more valleys. We experience a few events with favorable outcomes. It may be in the form of a new job you land, a business venture, you meet someone special in your life, that check in the mail finally comes, etc. It's a good feeling, but it's often short-lived. It's like the novelty of a new car that wears off once the new car smell has faded.

If you feel this way, or if you've ever felt this way, I want to give you some encouragement. It doesn't end there, and it certainly doesn't end with those teen and young-adult years. I absolutely hated high school and floated around somewhat lost throughout junior college and my young adult years. Even as an adult, once that temporary novelty of success has subsided, there's always more just around the corner. We just have to be open to it, and we have to be willing to fight for it.

So, how do you break away from these thoughts? It's like this force that keeps pulling us back once we've had a dose of something good in life. My answer is that you simply have to start living in the moment. When those successes come, enjoy them. Throw a party and celebrate. Take note of the event and find ways to replicate it, but don't get lazy! Don't lose the discipline it took to get to where you are. Don't stop doing. Don't stop pursuing. And as Journey instructs us, *Don't Stop Believing*.

My first album, though it wasn't a chart-buster, was a huge success to me. It was my very first album and something I had always dreamed of doing. I was 38 years old. What did I do after that? I immediately started working on new music for the next release. My only regret is I wish that wouldn't have taken me three years! So, what did I do after releasing my second album? I released a single later that same year and started working on *HMW II*. I'm telling you this because if you don't do anything with that momentum, it will surely fade. You have to continuously create momentum.

You have to embrace those working moments and allow the creativity to flow within you. How do you do that? Simple. By doing. Yes, you have to take that first step and act. This was tough for me to swallow. It's easy to sit back and daydream about the things we want to do and accomplish.

Some of us have what I call the "artists' curse" in that we tend to think that opportunities should be bestowed upon us and fall in our lap. We're convinced that our greatness should be realized, and if it's not, it's their (whoever 'they' are) loss. For this reason, most dreams never manifest. Why? Because there's no *action* that takes place.

I've recently read some interviews of writers and one of the common questions they get is in regard to writer's block. The many answers I've heard from successful writers is that you have to physically put the pen to the paper (or finger on the keyboard in today's world) and start writing. It doesn't matter if you feel creative or not, or if you're clueless as to what to write. You simply start doing.

Music is the same way. I can sit here and say that I don't feel inspired so I'm not going to bother going into the studio. Ninety-nine percent of the time it's not until I get into the studio and pick up my guitar that I get inspired, and it doesn't always hit me right away. I have to start playing those notes. Eventually, the progressions and melodies start to fall into place. It's almost like magic, but the you're the magician and you have to do the prep work to perform that magic. You may have to wave your wand a few times before the magic starts to happen.

I want to touch on another point. Many of us can be our own worst enemies constantly punishing ourselves for past mistakes. I've been extremely guilty of this over the years and still battle this today at times, though I've learned to tame those thoughts. This can indeed hold you back from success. It's one thing to learn from your mistakes (although these days I prefer to learn from someone else's mistakes), but you don't want to continuously stew in them.

A good friend once told me, and I'm sure this is quoted somewhere, that there's a reason why your windshield is so much bigger than your rearview mirror. This was many years ago and it was not a good time in my life, but in that moment, everything came to a screeching halt. That one hit me hard. Since then, I have used this line on others going through tough times and doubling up on self-punishment. I think it's impacted most everyone I've shared it with. It's an eye-opener and helps re-shift your focus on right now and what's ahead.

You can't move forward in life if you're constantly living in the past. Whether your past was filled with championships, being the most popular person, and you feel that the golden years have died and there's nothing exciting to look forward to, or if it was a dark past of nightmares turned into reality. If you remain stuck in those past times you'll never fulfill true destiny, which is to donate one hundred million dollars to me. Totally kidding there. Sort of.

I'll give you a quick exercise. Press pause...oh wait, this is a book, not a movie! Okay, mark your place in this book and go write down one goal that you want to start working towards (writing things down seems to bring them to fruition). It could be getting back into the gym, starting a blog that you've been talking about, learning a new instrument, taking a Yoga class, anything. Write it down (it can be more than one) and then write down a related task list that you will commit to doing this week.

If you're wanting to take some sort of lessons, that means your task will be researching the place or instructors, and calling to set up an appointment to check it out. If it's learning something new, order the book or tutorial you need, or start going through YouTube videos and create a playlist, then make a schedule to watch one or two per day and practice. Also give yourself a deadline for each task.

Another thing that can hold us back is people. Not people in general, but certain types of folks. Those that are driven by negativity do not want to see you, or anyone succeed.

Have you ever been around someone that you're afraid to share any good news with because they always fire back with something negative to bring you back down? I've experienced similar instances within the world of fitness and bodybuilding. Someone will walk by with a great physique and you'll hear someone else mumble things like "Oh, he or she's on steroids" or "They're just gifted with good genetics. If I had those genetics…blah, blah, blah."

Whether those are true or not, why does it matter? Then they'll start scrutinizing every part of their physique. Why can't they just acknowledge that the person is in good shape, or jacked, and let that be it? Perhaps not saying anything at all would suffice. I prefer the latter if the former isn't sincere. Sometimes you have to clean out your friends list. You have to do a purge. Get rid the negative people in your life, or at least limit your time with those people.

You see, our society seems to thrive off negativity. Just turn on the TV. Especially the news. They're not telling us about the missionaries that just helped rebuild a village in a poverty-stricken land or the group who just fed the homeless. They're not telling us about the counselor that talked someone out of taking their own life, or the police officer that just put his or her life on the line to rescue someone from an unspeakable crime. Nope, you won't hear about that kind of stuff. The bulk of what we will be presented with is downright bad news.

That's not to get you down. It's simply so that we can acknowledge that there's a layer of crap we must rise above. It's easy to get pulled into that cloud of negativity, which will only seep into our lives and ultimately control what we do and don't do. We must cut that out of our lives and, yes, this will be cheesy: turn that frown upside down.

The next step is to start surrounding yourself with positive people. Yeah, you knew that was coming. Seriously, start building relationships with those that can complement your character, and you, theirs. Now, I'm not saying to find a bunch of fans to blow smoke up your rear. I've always thought that was an odd saying…I mean, where would the smoke go? It has to come out somewhere, right? Your nose? Ears?

We ultimately become the type of people we surround ourselves with. It's not always intentional. It happens more within the subconscious realm. I'm not saying ditch your friends and join a millionaire's club. Rather, make a point to surround yourself with positive people and people that are taking action to achieve their goals.

Another suggestion is to find a mentor. This is something that I've come across frequently in reading about successful entrepreneurs. Even Arnold Schwarzenegger admits that there's no such thing as a self-made person. Arnold had many mentors and people that held him accountable resulting in the multiple ongoing successes throughout his life. Speaking of Arnold, I highly recommend *Total Recall: My True Unbelievable Life Story.* That's such a fascinating read, especially if you're an Arnold fan.

This may have seemed like a strange and off-topic chapter for this book. I thought about pulling it, but it may very well be the most important part for some. We all have dreams and things that we're passionate about, and we should pursue those dreams with all our might. It's what makes us who we are. And if we don't pursue these things, we're not living to our fullest, and we're cheating the world out of something very special that we have to offer.

I'm going to totally change gears in the next chapter. I'm going to give you something to apply the "doing" to that we talked about in this chapter, so get ready!

Heavy Metal Workout Philosophies

'I command you to grow!'

- CT Fletcher

The album series is called *Heavy Metal Workout* for a reason. Well, two reasons: it's heavy metal music, and it's made for working out. With that said, let's dive into some weight training concepts, and some actual workouts will follow.

I want to cover some of the workout philosophies I adhere to. I would imagine most of these can be found in Arnold's *Encyclopedia of Bodybuilding*, but it will be with my own twist based on my personal experiences over the years.

I realize that you may or may not work out on a regular basis. I'll try to keep this at a level everyone can understand. If you've been lifting for a while, you'll more than likely be familiar with these techniques. If you're not a gym-goer or you're new to the weights, hang in there, and Facebook me with any questions - https://www.facebook.com/jasonstallworthmetal/. This section will hopefully provide you with some good pointers and motivation before you jump in.

I'll also say this: most everything regarding types of workouts and concepts will work, but there are techniques that may work better than others. Also keep in mind that what works for you now may not work as well later. Our bodies change, our muscles adapt, and there are other elements that may impact the way our bodies respond to certain programs. Oftentimes the change doesn't have to be extreme, and it may even be temporary. One thing I've learned is that you have to shock your muscles with something a little different now and then in order to progress. You'll see this in one of the two workouts I provide in the next chapter.

So why do I feel weight training is so important? When I first started, I didn't think of any benefits beyond cosmetic. I later came to find that carrying lean muscle helps your body burn fat more efficiently. I also started to see the functional benefits of lifting weights. I became better at things that involved manual intervention. Unfortunately, helping friends move was one of those. Not so much a benefit, I would say.

More than anything, I noticed the psychological benefits of weight training. It's a tremendous confidence builder. As you know, this was a big thing for me. With lifting weights, you simply feel better overall as opposed to not using your muscles.

Alright, weight training principles. What are they? I'm going to start with breaking this up by body part: chest, back, legs, shoulders, and arms. Again, this is all from my own perspective and I'll keep it at a high level. I'm not trying to rewrite the many books that talk about this stuff, but there is a lot of ground to cover here.

Need to Get Something Off My Chest

When I see or hear the word "chest", the first thing that comes to mind is Arnold Schwarzenegger. He was known for his huge, fan-shaped chest. Lou Ferrigno, aka The Incredible Hulk, is another one that comes to mind, also a classic bodybuilder from that era. I recall a quote from an old bodybuilding magazine stating that Lou Ferrigno's chest enters the room five minutes before he does. Ah, I love bodybuilding puns. There's so many, and they're hilarious.

A huge chest is built with pressing movements. There are some pressing matters to tend to here. Okay, I'll stop. You're pushing weight away from your body, specifically your chest in this case.

Bench press is the primary exercise for building your chest muscles. It's also a common exercise for measuring strength. How many times have you heard "How much can you bench?", or even better, "I used to be able to bench press (insert some insane number here)."

For starters, strength is relative. I'm going off on a tiny tangent here, but I want you to always remember that the weights aren't about you trying to be better than someone else. In fact, don't compare yourself to others in the gym, or in any aspect. The weights are all about you against you. You're creating a more optimal version of yourself with every workout. It's a journey. Push hard and enjoy the journey.

Going back to chest, I find that incline exercises, such as incline bench press, incline dumbbell press, and incline dumbbell flyes, are great exercises to build both muscle mass and to shape your chest. It's important to hit the muscle from multiple angles.

Regular bench press with a barbell or dumbbells, mixed with incline movements, will give you a fully developed chest. Decline presses can also be thrown in, but I know some gyms do not have a decline bench. I've done decline exercises in the past, but rarely do them these days. I'm not against the decline, I just get plenty of results from flat and incline bench presses.

Chest training is simple. You have presses and flyes. While the types of chest presses we just discussed are pushing the weight away from your chest, flyes are a bit different. Think of flyes as hugging a big tree (Hey, I like huggie wuggies!). It's fair to say you should start with presses, and do more presses than flyes. I usually do a few sets of one flye exercise at the end of my chest workout if I'm doing a bodybuilding-style workout. If I'm training for more power and strength, I'll focus on bench presses, and may throw in a few sets of flyes every other week or so.

Flyes help stretch the muscle and are great for toning and shaping the chest, so don't leave them out completely.

Don't Worry Bro, I've Got Your Back

Over the years, back has become my favorite upper body muscle to train. The funny thing is, I didn't do much for back in my early years of working out. I was only doing a couple of exercises, none of which were core mass building exercises. Like Cher said, "If I could turn back time."

Seriously, I wish I had started out doing deadlifts and rows twice a week. But you live and learn, and I eventually integrated those into my routine.

Back is a super complex muscle, and like me in my younger years of weightlifting, many people have a hard time feeling those muscles working and getting a pump back there. Training back takes a lot of mental focus and homing in on technique in order to make those muscles do the work. You really have to zone in on every rep. I'll talk about sets and reps later. It's a mental state of extreme focus.

Whereas your chest is worked from pressing movements or pushing, back is worked with pulling exercises. So rather than pushing weight away from your body, you're pulling the weight towards your body. This movement activates those back muscles.

There are quite a few common exercises done for back, and plenty beyond the basics. The core type of exercise for building a thick and wide back is rows. For mass, barbell rows, also known as bent over rows, are the key. Other types of rows include dumbbell rows, and seated rows. These are done on a cable machine, and there's a variety of rowing machines. You can even reverse or change your grip on some of these exercises to hit different angles of your back muscles.

You also have exercises where you pull the weight down towards your chest from above you. These are called lat pull-downs and are done on a cable machine. They mimic the movement of pull-ups, which is also a great back-builder. I've recently started doing pull-ups at the end of my workouts two to three times a week.

It would be a sin to leave out what many consider the king of back exercises: deadlifts. This exercise is simply picking up raw weight from the floor and will build slabs of muscle. Although deadlifts are often done on back day, they're not limited to being just a back exercise. Deads practically work your entire body.

Just Pulling Your Legs

This is the most complained about day of the week. And no, it's not Monday. It's leg day. It's also, or at least it should be, your most brutal workout. Why? Legs are a huge muscle group.

Contrary to what you may have heard or read, you can develop muscular legs even if you aren't genetically gifted. What's the secret? Time and consistency. I guess patience comes along with that as well. I say this all from personal experience of being a skinny kid back in those days. I've also witnessed people with not-so-great genetics build an impressive set of wheels.

Squats and leg presses are going to be your foundation for building and developing your leg muscles. There are many other leg exercises, but those are going to be the most important. Don't skip them.

One thing I'll say about leg training is they respond really well to high volume workouts, meaning a lot of sets and reps. Don't be afraid to do more. I've personally found that my legs respond better to higher reps rather than going super heavy. I try not to go below 12 reps on anything for legs, with the exception of squats, when I'm training for strength and power.

The typical bodybuilding workout will have you training each muscle once a week. Of course, there are other theories, philosophies, and techniques that differ from that. Regardless, I prefer to train legs twice a week. My second leg workout may not include as much volume, but I want to stimulate those muscles more than once a week.

Think about how much time you spend on your upper body. There's probably at least three days a week between chest, back, shoulders, and arms. That's assuming you throw arms in with the other upper body muscles, such as chest and triceps, or back and biceps, which are common methods.

You spend all that energy on upper body and only one day a week on the largest muscle group of all: your legs. So, don't be afraid to do more for your lower body. I've even seen some people, and I've tried this myself in the past, split up quads and hamstrings, training them on separate days.

If you're just starting out with weight training, hit those legs hard. If they grow fast, that's awesome. If not, be consistent and give it time. Like in Wayne's World, "If you book them, they will come."

For legs, "If you train them hard, they will grow."

The Weight of the World on My Shoulders

One muscle group that certainly stands out, even with a shirt on, is shoulders. Big round shoulders give you that three-dimensional look. Another term for shoulders often heard is delts. With that comes a pun: "This is the hand (or the workout) you've been dealt."

Alright, I probably got some "boos" on that one.

You can work your shoulders from many angles through various types of lateral raises with both dumbbells and machines. Overall, shoulder mass will come from pressing exercises. I think of seated barbell presses to shoulders, as bench press is to chest. It's a compound exercise and you're pressing raw weight over your head. That's not an easy task.

One thing to keep in mind is that your shoulders get some work on chest and back day. When you're performing pressing exercises for chest, you're also incorporating your front and side delts to some degree. When you're working back, your rear delts are assisting. That doesn't mean you should slack on your shoulder workouts, but I personally tend to do less volume on shoulder day for that reason.

I usually lump in what's considered beach muscles on shoulder day. Those are called traps, but the accurate term is trapezius. Those are the muscles between your head and shoulders, and they make your neck look thicker kind of like the Hulk! I love the Hulk.

Those muscles also get some stimulation when training back, especially with rows and deadlifts. I know some that don't train traps at all. I sometimes go through phases where I don't train them directly.

When I do a workout for traps, I usually only do one exercise for them, and I typically train traps on shoulder or back day as a finishing move. The two most common exercises for them are barbell and dumbbell shrugs. A had a friend that called them "why nots" because of the movement that looks like you're shrugging your shoulders asking, "why not".

A Call to Arms

"Pardon me, but I don't believe they allow guns in here."

"We're going to the gun show!"

"The snack bar is that way (flexing a double biceps pose as you're pointing)."

"'You're looking armed and dangerous."

Yes, the arm puns never cease. Arms are fun to train because most people can get a pump very quickly with just a couple of sets. A lot of guys and girls alike will grab a quick arm workout and throw on a "smedium" shirt before they go out on a Friday night.

There's no doubt that having a good set of biceps and triceps is impressive. The thing I will harp on with arms is I see many doing multiple sets for biceps but not much for triceps. Your triceps make up most of your overall arm mass, so make sure you give them their due attention. Otherwise, you'll look funny and disproportioned.

I do have a Chuck Norris tank top that says, "Curls Bring the Girls!'"

A gift from my wife. I guess it worked!

Explaining Sets and Reps

This is mainly for the new folks but feel free to hang around because I'm going to get into some more depth here in explaining sets and reps.

It may be easier to start by defining what reps are. If you were to pick up a dumbbell and curl it from the starting position to the ending position, and back to the starting position, you would have just completed one rep. Do that same movement seven more times and you'll have a total of eight reps. Hopefully I got that right. I suck at math.

A rep is basically the act of performing a movement from start to finish. With weight training, it's ideal to perform several reps. I'll go further into that soon, but let's now move on to sets.

A set is one series of reps. So, if you were to take that dumbbell and do eight reps and then put the dumbbell back down, you would have just completed one set. It's common to rest anywhere from thirty seconds to over a minute before doing another set. The typical bodybuilding workouts have you performing three to four sets per exercise. If you're powerlifting or doing heavy sets where strength is the primary goal, you may rest a lot longer between sets.

I want to dive a little deeper here and chat about training volume. I often hear the debates on how many sets and reps should be done, and what's ideal for building muscle. There are many theories on this. It's been said by many bodybuilders that the muscle building rep range is anywhere from eight to twelve reps. This allows you to lift heavy enough weight while keeping the muscle under tension long enough to stimulate it.

As far as sets, I tend to stick to three sets for smaller muscles and four or more sets for larger muscles. That's sort of standard; however, I'm constantly making subtle changes so there's no hard-coded rules in place.

I recall reading Jay Cutler's (former four-time Mr. Olympia) answer to the question of sets and reps. He stated that there's no magical number of sets and reps that will make you grow. From my own experience, he's right, but there are some guidelines that tend to hold true.

If you're training with great intensity, you may do less sets. There's a method called high intensity training which takes each set to failure. If you're truly going all out, you won't be able to do another set. In this method, one or two working sets per exercise is common. This method is believed to completely exhaust the muscle.

On the flip side, many are big fans of high volume training over high intensity. It doesn't mean their workouts aren't intense, but they're not at the level as I just described. With this type of training, you can pump out more sets. High volume training is said to pump more blood into the muscle, which can lead to bigger muscles.

On a side note, your muscles don't grow while you're working out in the gym. The growth happens during the recovery process.

Like many, I alternate between various training methods. I may go through several weeks of high volume then switch to high intensity for a few weeks. For the most part, I'm somewhere in between. At the moment, I'm in a strength training phase focusing more on bench press, squats, and deadlifts, doing those exercises several times a week. Three months from now I may doing high volume workouts. It's also important to listen to your body. It will tell you when it's time to switch things up a little.

Rep range is another point of debate. I mentioned earlier that the standard muscle building rep range is between eight and twelve reps, but it's good to play around with different rep ranges. For example, I get better results in my legs from higher reps. I'll often do twenty-rep sets on leg press.

For strength gains, the lower reps work because you're lifting more weight, and the only way to get stronger is to lift more weight. Strength doesn't always equate to bigger muscles from a cosmetic perspective. Though strength and muscle go hand-in-hand, one will precede the other, and that's dependent upon your training style which should be catered to your personal goals.

I'm truly a middle-of-the-road type of guy. My style is considered *power building*. For most of my workouts throughout the year, I tend to go heavy with a compound exercise in the beginning by doing a reverse pyramid: going up in weight each set; this allows for a thorough warm up. The remaining exercises in my workouts will be within that eight to twelve rep range.

For those heavy compound exercises, I also do the "5 x 5" and "5-3-1" strength training methods.

With sets and reps, there are some techniques that you can use to increase intensity and volume all in one. We'll get into a few of those next.

Drop Sets

A drop set is performing a set and immediately doing another set with less weight. You're staying on the same exercise for this method. A good rule of thumb is to decrease the weight by thirty to forty percent on the drop. This will allow you to attain close to the same amount of reps as your initial set, doubling your volume for the entire set.

Drop sets can also serve as a time saver in the gym. It's a two-for-one concept, and can even be more if you prefer to keep dropping, such as a triple drop set.

There are several ways you can use drop sets but I prefer to use them towards the end of my workouts. This is when I want to end with that burn and pump. Drop sets will indeed grant you an extreme pump.

Of course, you can also do an entire workout using drop sets. This has the potential to cut your workout time practically in half. Here's an example of using drop sets for a biceps workout:

- Preacher curls: 2 sets x 8 reps, 1 drop set
- Dumbbell Hammer Curls: 2 sets x 10 reps, 1 drop set

This is how I often use drop sets. I'll perform a couple standard sets and do the third and final set with a drop set. The two standard sets allow you to push a decent amount of weight.

If I do drop sets for a larger muscle group, I'll save them for the end of the workout. If you do them in the beginning, you'll zap your strength and won't be able to lift as much with the preceding exercises. It's a great finishing move. Remember the "finishing moves" from *Mortal Combat*? That's what you'll say to your biceps in this case: "Finish them!"

By the way, Baraka was my favorite! He has those cool swords. I would play my uncle and cousin with Baraka and say, "A little off the ears?"

Supersets

Like drop sets, supersets is another two-for-one concept. Doing them can grant shorter workouts as well as workouts with more volume. They can also help increase intensity. So what exactly is a superset?

A superset is going from one exercise to another with no rest between those sets. Let's say you're training legs and you want to superset leg extensions with leg curls. You would do one set of leg extensions and immediately go into a set of leg curls. That round would count as one superset. Do a couple more of those and you'll feel it for sure.

You can do an entire workout using supersets or you may just want to implement this technique as one part of your workout. I'll give two examples below using back workouts.

Full Superset Workout

- Bent Over Rows *superset* with Pull-ups: 4 sets x 8-10 reps
- Seated Rows *superset* with Lat Pulldowns: 3 sets x 12 reps

Workout Implementing Supersets

- Bent Over Rows: 3 sets x 8 reps
- Dumbbell Rows: 3 sets x 10 reps
- Lat Pulldowns *superset* with Dumbbell Pullovers: 3 sets x 12 reps

If you're going for a shorter intense workout, the first full superset workout should suit you well. You may also be burning more calories with this type of workout simply because you're moving more and for longer durations with no rest. The muscle also stays under tension longer collectively. This is good for the pump.

For strength training, you'll want to do something like the second workout I listed. You can integrate supersets into your workout rather than doing them for your entire workout. If you're supersetting, you obviously won't be as strong on some of your lifts, especially the second exercise. So, hitting heavy weights in the beginning and saving supersets for that final round of exercises makes the most sense in this case.

I can't stress enough the time-savings in the gym that you get from supersets. You can do your workout in literally half the time with this method. It's quite convenient. So if it's one of those days where you only have twenty minutes or so, you can bang out a full workout by doing supersets. On that note, "I don't have time" is no longer a valid excuse. I recall my good friend Tom-Tom once saying to me, "You have time for what you make time for."

Pretty powerful quote.

The only drawback is you need to hog two machines. So if your gym is busy, or you are going at primetime, you may run into some issues trying to do supersets.

Rest-Pause Sets Technique

Rest-pause sets are brutal. It's one of my favorite muscle building techniques. If you want to completely exhaust your muscles, do a rest-pause set.

So, what is a rest-pause set? It's where you perform a set, then rest for about seven to ten seconds followed by another set. But here's the kicker: you don't change or lower the weight. You're using the same amount of weight. It doesn't make sense, does it?

Let's say you get twelve reps the first round. Once you rest that seven to ten seconds, you're only going to get about half of those reps on the second round, depending on the exercise. You can even do another round, rest another seven to ten seconds and go again, which you can expect an extremely low number of reps at that point.

Here's a view of how this works (we'll use rope press-downs for triceps as an example):

- Set 1 x 10-12 reps
  - 7 second rest
- Set 2 x 5-7 reps
  - 10 second rest
- Set 3 x 2-4 reps

The number of reps there aren't set in stone. That's just an example. You're going to be pushing as many as you possibly can. In this specific example, you're doing up to a total of twenty-three reps. That's one giant set with a lotta reps!

There are several ways to approach rest-pause sets. You could use them for your entire workout, but I don't recommend it. I know that may sound soft but it's too taxing on the body unless you're going for an extremely short workout.

I'll give two examples of ways to utilize rest-pause sets in your workout:

Rest-pause Workout on Final Sets of Each Exercise
- Seated Barbell Shoulder Press

- 3 sets x 8 reps, rest-pause on final set
- Lateral Raises
  - 3 sets x 10 reps, rest-pause on final set
- Upright Rows
  - 3 sets x 10 reps, rest-pause on final set

Rest-pause Workout on One (final) Exercise

- Seated Barbell Shoulder Press
  - 3 sets x 8 reps
- Lateral Raises
  - 3 sets x 10 reps
- Upright Rows
  - 2 rest-pause sets

I must mention, and this should be obvious, that if you're doing rest-pause sets for any type of free weight exercise, you absolutely need a spotter. Especially if they're exercises like barbell press or bench press where there's the possibly of the weight crushing you.

Negative Reps

This is one of the few times when a negative is actually positive. Do you want muscle growth? Strength gains? Do some negative reps.

Negatives are basically focusing on the descent of the rep. That's the most difficult part of the rep. With negatives, you control the weight rather than allowing the resistance to move the weight towards its natural position.

Negatives are often used for building strength as it allows your muscles to get used to handling heavier weights. If you can control 315 pounds, then you can probably power up 345 pounds. They're also effective for building dense muscle by allowing you to dig deep into those muscle fibers.

Let's use bench press as an example. At the starting position, your arms are straight above you holding the bar over your chest. When you start to let the weight descend towards your chest, lower the bar slowly. This means you're pressing against the resistance of the weight, forcing the descent towards your chest to be gradual, controlling how long that takes.

Here are the steps in bullet-point style:

1. Make sure you have a spotter!
2. Lay on the bench and grab the bar.
3. Lift the bar off the rack.
4. Flexing your muscles and keeping your core tight, slowly bring the bar towards your chest.
5. Control the descent of the weight, taking three or more seconds before it gets to your chest.
6. Once the bar gets to your chest, use explosive power to lift the weight back to the starting position.

There are different opinions on how long you should take on the descent. I personally take about three seconds. That's long enough to know that you're truly controlling the weight, thus making the muscle work harder.

You don't typically do this for every set or rep. For heavy compound exercises, I'll often perform the last rep or two as a negative. That would look something like this going up in weight each set:

Negatives on Final Set

- 1st set: 10 normal reps
- 2nd set: 8 normal reps
- 3rd set: 4 normal reps, 1-2 negative reps

Negative reps are especially great on machines because you don't necessarily need a spotter. If your gym has Hammer Strength machines, do negative reps on those. They mimic the movement of free weight exercises quite nicely but have the feel of free weights as they're plate-loaded as opposed to cables and pins.

I encourage you to incorporate negative reps into your workouts, especially on lifts you want to get stronger on. Just make sure you have a trusted spotter on the free weight exercises. The last thing you want is the bar stuck on your chest. Been there; it's not cool.

Weight Training Techniques

There are many other weightlifting techniques and ways to make your workouts more intense. Of course, many concepts are old ones that have been reinvented with a twist or new name. You can take just about anything and modify it to your liking.

Try alternating these techniques. For example, integrate rest-pause sets for a few weeks and then switch to supersets for another few weeks. Another option is to use specific techniques for certain muscles or exercises for a while. The possibilities are endless.

Just like there's no magic number of sets or reps, there's no mystical technique that's going to grant substantial results overnight. The keys to building muscle are intensity and consistency. You have to want it bad enough, and you have to be patient enough to stick with it. It must become part of who you are.

Heavy Metal Workouts

'Everybody wants to be a bodybuilder, but nobody wants to lift no heavy-ass weights.'

- Ronnie Coleman

Now let's dig into the meat and potatoes. Actually, that sounds like a great idea, in a literal sense. I do love to eat!

This book wouldn't be complete without an actual workout program. We've covered some basic weight training principles and techniques you can use in the gym. It's now time to apply them.

I'll give you two different types of workout programs here. The first one caters to building muscle mass. I know that sounds generic but that's the core reason why many of us start lifting weights. We simply want to build muscle, and get big and strong. This program covers the basis for gaining muscle, and we'll call it my *HMW Muscle Mass Workout*.

The second workout is more for getting lean and cut. The workouts are geared towards building lean muscle, but keeping your heart rate up throughout the workout. You won't be as strong with this type of workout, but you will get lean and you'll look good. We shall call this my *HMW Lean Muscle Workout*.

Since this isn't an actual workout book or full workout program, there's going to be some research you may want to do on your end. For example, if you're not familiar with some of the exercises listed, look them up on YouTube or ask a trainer at the gym. You can also substitute an exercise with a similar one, or just take the basis of the workouts I'm providing and use them as a platform to create your own workout plan. My goal here is to give you a starting point and a guide.

Happy lifting!

HMW Muscle Mass Workout - Weeks 1-4

In this workout program, you'll be lifting heavy weights using compound movements in the beginning of your workout. Compound movements are exercises like squats, deadlifts, bench press, barbell rows, just to name a few. These are multi-joint exercises (also called complex exercises), which means you're using multiple muscles. These exercises allow you to lift more weight thus overloading the muscle. This is part of the mass building effort.

As your workout progresses, you'll move to doing more repetitions, and you'll end your workout with isolated exercises. You're building a foundation for mass and strength while also fine-tuning your physique. This is a bodybuilding-style workout focused on building overall mass.

The *HMW Muscle Mass Workout* has you training four days per week. The schedule will look something like this:

Monday: Workout 1 - Back and Biceps

Tuesday: Workout 2 - Chest and Triceps

Wednesday: *Rest*

Thursday: Workout 3 - Legs

Friday: Workout 4 - Shoulders

Saturday & Sunday: *Rest*

Rest Between Sets: About a minute and a half for compound exercises and rep ranges under twelve, and 45 seconds to a minute for everything else.

You can switch these days up if you want. I wrote this based on the typical Monday through Friday work schedule. But feel free to change up the days to fit your schedule.

This is a two-phase workout plan, which will ultimately last for eight weeks, or longer if you choose to go through the program again. You'll do the same workouts each week for four weeks followed by a few changes in your workouts for the last four weeks. Making these changes will help keep your muscles growing. You shock the muscle by doing something different yet you're not straying off course from your complex muscle building exercises.

You could essentially do two rounds of this workout making it a twelve-week workout program. The second time around, you may choose to switch up the exercises a little more and create your own workout plan using this one as a guide.

The first four weeks consist of a lot of basic compound exercises. Hopefully you're already familiar with these. If not, you can look them up on the Internet or watch a YouTube video on how to do them. I'm a YouTube junkie and have learned so many things such as how to use recording software, how to fix things (I'm not handy at all), and yes, I've watched my fair share of workout videos. In fact, you may come across a few of my own workout videos.

The goal is mass. And to gain mass, you need resistance. So, you're starting out by lifting heavy and as you progress through the workout, you'll start pumping out more reps. There's no fancy techniques for these four weeks, just straight sets and reps.

While the *HMW Muscle Mass Workout* is along the lines of a typical bodybuilding workout, it could also be considered a *power building* workout as you can expect to get bigger and stronger.

Let's go over a few notes before starting the first few weeks of this *HMW Muscle Mass Workout*:

- The workouts below do not include warming up. Do a couple of warmup sets on the first exercise
- Make sure you have a spotter for the free weight exercises, especially for pressing movements
- Focus on contracting the muscle throughout the reps. In other words, don't just go through the motions
- Focus on going a little slower, 2-3 seconds, on the negative part of each rep

Now you're ready to hit the gym. The next few pages will cover each workout in detail. I suggest sticking to this first phase for four weeks. After that you can jump into the second phase of the *HMW Muscle Mass Workout* program, which is covered after this phase.

Exercise	Sets x Reps
Barbell Rows	4 x 10, 10, 8, 6
Deadlifts	3 x 10, 8, 6
Dumbbell Rows	3 x 8
Lat Pulldowns	3 x 10
Dumbbell Hammer Curls	3 x 8
Standing EZ Bar Curls	3 x 10

There's nothing that spells mass on back day more than rows and deadlifts. Talk about heavy metal! Those exercises are the foundation for a thick and wide back. You'll be going heavy on those first two exercises, especially on the final sets (six-rep sets).

These exercises for both back and biceps are basic movements proven to build muscle mass. It's one of those things where it doesn't matter what new workout trends are thrown at us. You just can't beat these exercises.

Though you're lifting heavy weights, don't break your form. You'll hear me say this a thousand times:

Don't just go through the motions, make the muscle do the work.

Flex your back muscles when you're pulling the weight towards you. And use the same principle for biceps. Flex that muscle once you get to the peak of the rep. It will make a "huge" difference.

Let me back up and harp a little on deadlifts. Make sure you know what you're doing here, and don't try to lift more weight than you can reasonably handle. Again, look up these exercises and see how to properly do them. It's not a bad idea to hire a trainer, or get someone experienced at the gym who understands your goals to watch your form. The same applies to barbell rows. The last thing you want is a lower back injury, so do your due diligence if you're uncertain. Proper form is key.

Exercise	Sets x Reps
Bench Press	4 x 10, 10, 8, 6
Incline Dumbbell Press	3 x 10, 8, 6
Dumbbell Flyes	3 x 10
Skull Crushers	3 x 8
Rope Pressdowns	3 x 10

It's day two and you may be a little sore from your back and bicep workouts, but today you'll be pushing, not pulling. It's all chest and triceps.

You may be wondering why you didn't start with chest. For many, the first workout of the week is on Monday, and Mondays are famous for being International Chest Day. Seriously, it seems every bench is taken on Mondays. That's one of the reasons why I have you training chest on day two. Another reason is that back is a larger muscle group than chest, so it's good to start out with back as your first workout of the week.

The concepts of this workout are the same as the first day for back and biceps. You're starting out with some basic compound exercises and you'll be going heavy. Since you're doing all free weights for chest, I recommend that you find a trusted spotter. If not, you can substitute these exercises with machines, but I've found that most people are willing to give you a spot. Just make sure they don't grab the bar when you start to struggle a little. They need to make you work for it.

I recall working out with a guy who would do this. As soon as you showed any sign of struggle he'd grab the bar and pull it up. As he was doing this, he'd be saying, "It's all you man, you've got this."

This killed my actual strength! My muscles weren't being pushed to the max and it was deceptive to my psyche. There's a fine balance with spotting; it's an art. I have a small handful of gym buddies I trust with this, and we help each other out.

HMW Muscle Mass Workout 3 - Legs

Exercise	Sets x Reps
Squats	4 x 8-10
Leg Press	4 x 12-15
Leg Extensions	4 x 12-15
Stiff-Leg Deadlifts	4 x 12-15
Seated or Standing Leg Curls	4 x 12-15

Ah, it's your favorite day of week, right? Leg day.

You'll notice that you're taking a different approach from the last two workouts. There's a little more volume and the reps are higher overall. For muscle growth, legs tend to respond better to high volume and more reps. If your goal is to gain more strength, you can lower the reps on squats and go heavier.

I've learned to love training legs over the years. This typically happens once you start seeing results. What changed for me is I increased the reps. Soon after, I started bumping up the overall training volume. I could go on all day about this, but volume and reps will work miracles for those stubborn quads and hamstrings.

I'm not saying don't go heavy. By no means is this a light-weight workout. Legs are powerful in nature. For example, even starting out as a beginner, you can lift far more weight on the leg press than you can on the bench press. So, you'll be pushing a decent amount of weight. That mixed with the high volume and higher reps will make your legs grow like weeds.

One thing I need to cover here is half-reps. Have you ever seen someone load up the leg press machine with as much weight as it can possibly hold only to go a few inches down before pressing it back up? That's not a rep. You need to go at least parallel before you start pressing the weight back up (same with squats). Half-reps will only build your ego, not your legs.

On that note, some will say drop all the way down to where your hamstrings touch your calves. There are different methods but going parallel is fine. Try dropping a little below parallel on the leg press though. That's the machine people tend to take shortcuts on. You want to make sure you get a good range of motion.

HMW Muscle Mass Workout 4 – Shoulders

Exercise	Sets x Reps
Seated Barbell Press	4 x 10, 10, 8, 6
Upright Rows	4 x 8
Barbell Shrugs	4 x 8
Lateral Raises	3 x 10

Shoulders are going to be your final workout of the week. You gave your upper body muscles a little break with a day off followed by a leg workout. So you should be somewhat fresh.

I don't do quite as much volume for shoulders simply because they get some stimulation from working chest and back. That doesn't mean you should skip them or skimp on them. Train them hard and heavy. But for me, shoulder day is somewhat abbreviated. If you feel that your shoulders need more work, feel free to add extra sets or exercises.

You're starting out with a pressing exercise and going heavy, seated barbell presses, also called military press and overhead press. These are tough. It's dead weight that you're lifting directly over your head which is the greatest angle of resistance. I do recommend a spotter here, the same as doing bench press. If not, you can substitute this exercise with a machine such as the Hammer Strength plate-loaded shoulder press. I'm a big fan of their machines.

The exercises thereafter are isolation exercises and they will help shape the muscle, giving you those rounded delts. Try slowing the reps down on these exercises. You will indeed feel the burn.

After the first four weeks of pushing and pulling some heavy weights, you should be feeling and looking pretty good. The exercises you have been doing build the foundation for gaining solid muscle mass. Are you ready for phase two of the *HMW Muscle Mass Workout*?

For the second phase, the exercises aren't going to change much, though there will be some slight shifts. We want to continue with compound exercises required for building mass and strength. The main changes will be a couple of techniques we're going to throw in during this phase.

You'll see some drop sets and rest-pause sets. I explained those in an earlier chapter, so go back and revisit if needed. The reason for bringing these techniques into the picture is to increase the intensity. You'll see an asterisk (*) at the bottom of each workout explaining these.

You'll also notice that the drop sets and rest-pause sets are done towards the end of your workouts, and on the final sets. This is a great way to finish your workout, forcing you to go out strong, so make sure you're mentally prepared for this. It's going to be one of those times where you feel like you have no gas left in the tank, but you have to bang out those last few reps. Push through; you'll surprise yourself.

You can refer to the same notes I mentioned in the first phase of the *HMW Muscle Mass Workout* a few pages back. They will apply in the same manner, and are fairly basic. Keep the reps strict. Don't just go through the motions, and focus on that negative portion of the rep. That's the part of the rep that really breaks down the muscle, resulting in more growth.

Phase two of mass training, here we come!

Exercise	Sets x Reps
Deadlifts	4 x 6-8
Barbell Rows	3 x 8
Reverse Grip Lat Pulldowns	3 x 10*
Seated Rows	3 x 12**
Standing Alternate Dumbbell Curls	3 x 10 *
Preacher Curls	3 x 12**

*Rest-pause set on final set

**Drop set on final set (reduce weight about 40%)

It's the night (or day) of the living dead! Another semi-poorly delivered gym pun Deadlifts - get it? It's worse when you explain the pun, right?

We're starting out with deadlifts here, and as I've already mentioned, I recommend that you do a couple of warm-up sets prior to jumping into your working sets. You may want to do a little dynamic stretching as well and re-read my excerpt at the bottom of the page for phase one of the *HMW Muscle Mass Workout* pertaining to deadlifts and form.

Deadlifts take a lot of mental focus and energy. And doing them first will allow you to go a bit heavier. Remember, deads were your second exercise during the first four weeks, phase one.

You'll be doing some rows after that, and I threw in a reverse grip exercise: lat pulldowns. This hits a different angle of your back than the regular lat pulldowns. I like to alternate the two.

You're doing two different exercises for biceps during phase two. But as you can see, they're standard exercises. I'm not into crazy exercises. I tend to stick to the basics. In my experience, those have worked best, especially for training arms.

Exercise	Sets x Reps
Incline Press	4 x 6-8
Dumbbell Press	4 x 10**
Incline Dumbbell Flyes	3 x 12**
Skull Crushers	3 x 10*
Rope Pressdowns	3 x 12**

*Rest-pause set on final set

**Drop set on final set (reduce weight about 40%)

I absolutely love incline exercises for chest, and that's what we're starting out with during phase two of the *HMW Muscle Mass Workout*. It's been said by many pro bodybuilders that you can't possibly have too much upper chest, and this is an area where many lack. Doing incline bench press first will prove to be a crucial part of your overall chest development.

Don't worry, you won't be neglecting the regular flat movement of bench press, but you'll be doing this movement with dumbbells instead of the barbell which you did incline dumbbell press during phase one. This helps you work different parts of the muscle; however, if your goal is to increase your regular bench press, feel free to change the workout accordingly. I promise, you won't hurt my feelings.

"I didn't know you had any feelings" - Dave Mustaine

After chest, your triceps should be warmed-up and primed. Now it's time to hit them directly. Skull crushers are a powerful exercise for building triceps. The range of motion and angle allows you to work the triceps fully. Grab a spotter for this one. The rope press downs you'll be doing have always been a great finishing move for triceps.

You may also notice that I have you doing more ending techniques in this workout. Rest-pause sets and drop sets seem to work well for chest and arms, allowing you to exhaust the muscle and leave the gym with an extreme pump.

II HMW Muscle Mass Workout 3 - Legs

Exercise	Sets x Reps
Leg Press	5 x 12-15
Front Squats	4 x 10
Leg Extensions	3 x 12*
Seated or Standing Leg Curls	3 x 12*
Dumbbell Lunges	4 x 12-15

Rest-pause set on ALL sets

It's the almighty leg day again. We're changing the first part of the workout for this phase. The first change is you'll be starting out with leg press instead of squats. I encourage you to play around with foot placement, mainly trying a closer stance as this hits the outer quads more. You can start with a close foot placement and gradually go out a little further apart each set thereafter. I never go too wide as I just don't feel I get as much out of the exercise with a super wide foot placement, although I can push more weight with a wider stance. So I would say don't go much wider than shoulder width. With leg press, you want to go with a stance where you feel your legs working harder over how much weight you can press. Remember, we're building muscles, not egos.

Front squats replace regular squats in this workout. These really target the quads and glutes. You won't be able to go as heavy. In fact, go super light at first if you're not used to doing front squats. Get your form down before you start adding weight. If your goal is to increase squat strength, feel free to continue with regular squats here instead of front squats. Again, it won't hurt my feelings! In fact I encourage you at some point to cater the workout plan I'm giving you to best suit your goals and dreams, "cause that's what dreams are made of" - Sammy Hagar, from the incredible 5150 album.

I have you hitting rest-pause sets for leg extensions and leg curls. This will add a substantial amount of volume to the overall workout. Challenge yourself here and really push yourself. You can pump out a lot more than you may think and you may find yourself going up in weight quickly on these exercises.

You'll end this workout with what many consider a brutal leg exercise: dumbbell lunges. You can do walking lunges if you have a large area, or stay in one spot. You can also do lunges with the barbell (same position as if you were doing squats).

II HMW Muscle Mass Workout 4 - Shoulders

Exercise	Sets x Reps
Seated Dumbbell Press	4 x 8-10**
Bent Over Raises	3 x 10
Lateral Raises	3 x 10
Dumbbell Shrugs	3 x 12**

**Drop set on final set (reduce weight about 40%)

Like phase one of the *HMW Muscle Mass Workout* program, shoulders will be your final workout of the week. I kept the same schedule, mainly because I prefer this schedule. Feel free to change it.

You'll be replacing seated barbell press with seated dumbbell press. And if you choose, you can do what's called Arnold presses. You won't be able to do as much weight, but you may find that you get a better pump with Arnold presses. Not to mention, anything with Arnold's name in it must be pretty effective and cool.

You can also substitute bent over lateral raises with the reverse pec-dec machine. This is done by facing the pec-dec machine, which is primarily used for chest flyes, and pulling the weight out away from you, which works your rear delts. Try both exercises and do what works best for you, or alternate them each week. I usually choose free weights over machines. It's just my personal preference.

If you feel that you need to add more volume to your shoulder workout, by all means, do so. I explained in phase one why I do less volume for shoulders. On top of that, I have decent natural shoulder development leaving me to have to focus more on back and legs.

HMW Lean Muscle Workout - 8 Weeks

The *HMW Lean Muscle Workout* program is more fast-paced and you'll stay moving. There's less rest between sets, and you'll be doing supersets and drop sets throughout most of your workouts. I'll explain why below.

This is a six day per week workout program. At a glance it may look exhausting, but the workouts may actually be shorter than the *HMW Muscle Mass Workout*. The key here is to do something active each day with only one day of rest. You want to keep your metabolism up, turning your body into a fat-burning machine.

Here's what the *HMW Lean Muscle Workout* schedule looks like:

Monday: Workout 1 - Chest and Back

Tuesday: Workout 2 - Legs

Wednesday: Workout 3 - Bodyweight and Core

Thursday: Workout 4 - Shoulders and Arms

Friday: Workout 5 - Legs

Saturday: Workout 6 - Bodyweight and Core

Sunday: *Rest and eat pizza (seriously, take a little break!)*

Rest Between Sets: About 45 seconds

If you need to switch the days around, that's fine, and if you feel you need a break in the middle of the week, that means you totally suck! I'm kidding! Seriously, take a break if you feel you need one. Listen to your body and just pick back up where you left off.

I used the term "lean muscle" because I don't care for the term "fat burning". In theory, the *HMW Lean Muscle Workout* will cater to just that: dropping those pounds and hardening your body. However, it will not be at the expense of losing muscle. The ultimate goal is to gain lean muscle while getting cut and conditioned. Yes, like that Van Halen song, we want the *Best of Both Worlds*.

As you may imagine, your nutrition plan is going to be a key driver in your progress, but I'm not going to touch on that part. I encourage you to do your own research. There are so many diet philosophies floating around out there. The truth is different diets work for different types of people. At the end of the day, just be sensible. The one tip I will give you is ditching processed foods and reducing sugars is a great first step. That on its own will work wonders in your physique and the way you feel.

You will indeed be lifting weights for this workout program. I mention this because many think that you have to do endless amounts of cardio to get lean. On the contrary, I'm a firm believer that the more muscle you have, the more efficiently your body can burn fat. On a side note, your workouts may feel more like a "strength training meets cardio" session. You'll be lifting, but you'll also be continuously moving which results in burning more calories.

The notes at the beginning of the *HMW Muscle Mass Workout* apply to the *HMW Lean Muscle Workout* program as well. However, I'll restate them below, so you don't have to go digging for it.

Notes:

- The workouts below do not include warming up. Do a couple of warmup sets on the first exercise
- Make sure you have a spotter on free weight exercises
- Focus on contracting the muscle throughout the reps. In other words, don't just go through the motions
- Focus on going a little slower, 2-3 seconds, on the negative part of each rep

The workouts may be tough. If you don't feel that they're tough, then make them tough! You can adjust the intensity according to your level and your personal goals, but don't go soft on yourself. Push yourself; you can do a lot more and go a lot further than you think.

One last note before we jump into the workouts: make a commitment to stick with this program for at least six weeks. I don't want to hear any excuses like "Well, uh, I just don't have time" or whatever.

Be dedicated and force yourself to get in the gym. Again, the workouts are shorter. Did I mention don't make excuses?

It's time to get lean, so get ready!

HMW Lean Muscle Workout 1 - Chest and Back

Exercise	Sets x Reps
Incline Bench Press *superset with below	3 x 10
Seated Rows	3 x 10
Dumbbell Press *superset with below	2 x 12
Barbell Rows	2 x 12
Pec Dec Flyes *superset with below	2 x 15
Lat Pulldown	2 x 15

We talked about supersets earlier, so if you need to revisit that section, please do. To quickly recap, a superset is when you go from one exercise immediately to another with no rest. That's one superset. After that, you'll want to rest for thirty to forty-five seconds before starting the next superset.

Since this is the first workout, I'm going to harp more on rest time. If you feel you're getting winded and need a few more seconds, take it. Supersets can be tough, especially if you're not in good cardiovascular shape. There's a balance between keeping your heart rate up and having enough juice to do the next set correctly and with intensity.

You're starting with what I consider one of the best exercises for developing your chest muscles: incline bench press. Once you finish that first set you're going to race over to the seated row machine and hit 10 reps for your back.

Training chest and back together will give your entire upper body an incredible pump, but it's also exhausting. If you're a guy, you're naturally going to try to go hard and heavy on chest, especially if it's International Chest Day…that never gets old! However, back is the largest upper body muscle so you should be pushing yourself hard on those exercises as well.

You'll also notice the reps climb up as you go through this workout, so the weight will naturally decrease. Once you get to the last round of exercises, you'll essentially be doing a thirty-rep set: fifteen reps of lat pulldowns immediately followed by fifteen reps of flyes. On that note, you may be a bit sore the next day so make sure you stretch those muscles after your workout and take your amino acids.

"Take your protein pills and put your armor on, ground control to Major Tom." - David Bowie

Exercise	Sets x Reps
Squats *superset with below	3 x 12
Seated Calves Raises	3 x 12
Leg Press *superset with below	3 x 12
Lying Leg Curls	3 x 12
Leg Extensions *superset with below	2 x 15
Stiff-Leg Deadlifts	2 x 15

Did I mention how much I love leg day? This is one of my favorite types of leg workouts, hitting a lot of different exercises that work various angles. Trust me, your legs will be exhausted after this workout. It's going to be brutal, but remember, don't just go through the motions on these exercises. Make sure you feel your leg muscles working. Legs are the largest muscle group in your entire body and they require more attention than what most are willing to give them.

Since squats take a ton of mental focus, I have you super setting squats with calf raises rather than another exercise for quads or hamstrings. This makes the most sense to me.

After squats, you're going to be hogging the leg equipment area for the next twenty minutes or so. My suggestion is train in the early morning when your gym opens. There's a smaller gym crowd at that time.

The truth about legs: **If you train your legs hard, you'll force the results to come**.

This doesn't mean you have to be puking after leg day, but you may wobble a little as you're leaving the gym.

I recommend stretching after every workout. For legs, stretch even more. It's also okay to walk or ride the recumbent bike for a little while. This will help you recover from your workout.

Exercise	Sets x Reps
Pull-ups *superset with below	3 x 10
Push-ups	3 x 10
Leg Raises	2 x 12
Rope Crunches	2 x 12
Bicycle Kicks	30 seconds x 2
Planks	30 seconds x 2

In this workout, you're not lifting any weights. It's all bodyweight exercises and core training. You're starting out with some good ole fashioned pull-ups and push-ups. You can use the assisted pull-up machine if you need to. But I encourage you to do as many pull-ups with your bodyweight as possible. You can mix the two as well. For example, if you can only do two or three bodyweight pull-ups, do the rest of the reps using assisted pull-ups.

For push-ups, if you can't do regular ones, you can start with knee push-ups, but try to do as many regular ones as possible before going to the knee push-ups. If you're already good at pull-ups and push-ups, you can add more reps. The goal is to do any many as you can with good form.

For core, you're starting out with some abdominal exercises. The leg raises can be performed on the dip bar with your back against the pad holding yourself up with your forearms. Rope crunches can be done on any cable machine with the ropes. I prefer this exercise to regular crunches as this doesn't seem to involve your lower back as much as regular crunches do. At least that's the case for me.

You'll be finishing your workouts with planks, which is a pose that you hold. You can increase the time as you get better at them. Also, don't be afraid to throw in some Yoga. Yoga is something I recently started doing and I wish I had started this years ago. It's increased my flexibility and eliminated my lower back pain. Yoga is magical! And so is Yoda, for that matter!

As always, if you have questions about these exercises, look up a video to see how they're performed.

Exercise	Sets x Reps
Seated Dumbbell Press *superset with below	4 x 12
Lateral Raises	4 x 12
Rope Pressdowns *superset with below	2 x 10
Dumbbell Hammer Curls	2 x 10
Seated Overhead Dumbbell Extensions *superset with below	2 x 12
Preacher Curls	2 x 12

Except for rope press downs, this workout can be done with all free weights, mostly dumbbells. That said, feel free to substitute any exercises as needed. I'm personally a fan of free weights over machines, but everything has its place.

I don't have you doing as much volume for shoulders simply because you get a lot of shoulder work from training chest and back (I covered this in the *HMW Mass Workout*). However, since there are only two exercises, I bumped up the number of sets for each to four.

Get ready for an extreme pump in your arms once you finish shoulders. Going back and forth between triceps and biceps will blow your arms up like crazy! It's a great feeling.

On the biceps and triceps exercises, make sure you're flexing the muscle at the peak of each rep. This goes for all of these workouts in the *HMW Lean Muscle Workout* plan, but especially arms. Your arms will literally grow right there in the gym. It's time for a smedium shirt!

HMW Lean Muscle Workout 5 - Legs

Exercise	Sets x Reps
Leg Press (close foot placement) *superset with below	3 x 10
Leg Press (regular foot placement)	3 x 10
Seated Leg Curls *superset with below	3 x 12
Standing Calve Raises	3 x 12
Dumbbell Lunges *superset with below	2 x 15
Leg Extensions	2 x 15

Get ready to do something a little different for legs. You're starting out with leg press. The twist is you're super setting leg press with leg press. So, what's so special about that? You're changing your foot placement.

This technique, which I don't have a name for, is one of my favorites for leg day. You'll begin with a close foot placement. I have you starting with that first because you can't do as much weight with that stance. After ten reps, you'll rack the weight, widen your foot placement to about shoulder width, unlock the weight, and pump out ten more reps. Make sure the leg press is locked before you change your foot placement.

This method will pump a ton of blood into the muscle and will set the tone of intensity for the rest of your workout.

Most of the exercises after leg press are standard. I don't do anything crazy or trendy. I stick with the basics that have been time-tested over decades for building muscle. I'm not against innovation and trying new things, but when it comes to weight training, the basics simply work best. You'll hear me preach that message more than once.

Exercise	Sets x Reps
Reverse Grip Pull-ups *superset with below	3 x 10
Dips	3 x 10
Decline Sit-ups	2 x 12
Rope Crunches	2 x 12
Bicycle Kicks	30 seconds x 2
Planks	30 seconds x 2

You're ending the week with another bodyweight and core workout. Although you'll be doing pull-ups again, your grip will be reversed to an underhand grip. This works the lower part of your back muscles, your lats.

As with the prior bodyweight and core workout, use the assisted machine for both pull-ups and dips if you must, but focus on getting better at both of these exercises. When you can do ten to twelve reps of pull-ups and dips with your bodyweight, you can do more reps or start slowing down the reps, making them harder.

After pull-ups and dips, you'll move on to the exercises that focus on your core. I have you doing the same core exercises as the prior workout. Feel free to change these up if you prefer to substitute them with other exercises. I was too lazy to look up more core exercises (there's so many!). Hey, just being honest. *Almost Honest* - cool Megadeth song from their *Cryptic Writings* album. I had to look that up. I almost typed *Countdown to Extinction* album instead. I would've been extremely wrong.

You Finished the HMW Workout Program - What Now?

Anytime you finish a workout program, it's not a bad idea to back off a little before going into another workout program or repeating the one you just finished. Some choose to take a week off from the gym. That's certainly an option and it won't hurt to give your body a break. I prefer to do a deloading workout instead.

Deloading is where you don't workout with as much intensity or as much volume. In short, it's sort of just showing up to the gym and going through the motions, or you can think of it as getting a quick pump.

You can do this for a week or two. A week typically works for me, and you may only train two or three days that week. You could do Monday, Wednesday, and Friday, or even better, do deloading workouts Monday through Wednesday and take off until the following Monday. That gives you five days off from the gym.

Here's a deload workout plan for three days:

- Day 1: Chest, Shoulders and Triceps
- Day 2: Back and Biceps
- Day 3: Legs

Pick two or three exercises for your larger muscles and one for smaller muscles. Maybe do two to three sets of ten reps for each without going to failure. You're working out, but not training super-intense, giving your body and muscles a little break.

After a short break, you may decide to do the same workout program again. Or better yet, and this is something that I greatly encourage, you can adjust the program you just finished and customize it to your specific goals.

I want you to understand something about workout programs in general. Most of them will work regarding producing results. That's given that you follow the plan, of course. When you do something you're not used to doing, your body and muscles will naturally respond to that. I'm not necessarily saying that you should change your workout plan for the mere sake of changing it. If what you're doing is working for you, by all means continue. But at some point, you're more than likely going to plateau, and you'll want to switch things up to break through.

Workout programs are guides. Yes, you can follow them to the tee initially, but take notes as you go. When you're done, go back and review those notes and see what worked best for you and what wasn't so great. Chew up the meat and spit out the bones. Make the necessary changes to that workout plan so that it will be even more effective.

Do Something Daily and Stay Active

'If you're capable of sending a legible text message between sets, you probably aren't working hard enough.'

- **Dave Tate**

Working out isn't limited to lifting weights, although the weights have made up the bulk (Yes, pun intended.) of my workouts over the years. On that note, I will also talk about some other types of training. At the end of the day, doing something is better than doing nothing. But I do recommend some sort of resistance training to build lean muscle.

Let me just say this now:

Do something active every day.

Even if it's a twenty-minute walk, ten minutes of stretching, or Yoga. Heck, maybe you like to dance, so go cut a rug. Do something. Move your body.

There are so many activities you can get involved in that will help you stay fit. I suggest choosing something you enjoy doing. I've heard people complain about working out at the gym. My advice is a mix between "stop making excuses and do it anyway" and "don't do it; find another activity". Either way, doing nothing should *never* be an option.

For some, the gym is intimidating. Hey, I totally get that. Remember in the first part of this book reading about how easily intimidated I was?

I remember a funny story: I was in junior college working out at the YMCA. I was in another town, Brewton, Alabama, staying with my aunt, uncle, and cousins during those years. My cousin and I were at the gym, and he was a bit bigger and stronger than me back then. Some of his old high school football buddies showed up. I remember having 185 pounds on the bench press, but I could only push it for a few reps. One of his buddies tauntingly walked over to the bench and said, "Hey, let me try that…but I don't know if I can get it as many times as you did!'"

He pumped out like twelve or so reps like it was nothing. I thought "Dude, what a jerk!"

Intimidation is not much of a factor these days. There are all kinds of gyms, and a common theme is "judgement free zones". I used to laugh at that concept, but I had to stop myself. This may be the one thing that gets someone in the gym and on the path to getting healthy. If that's the case, I'm all for it.

A great form of exercise is practicing martial arts. I grew up being a huge Bruce Lee fan (Seriously, as an '80s kid, who wasn't?). I remember watching *Kung Fu Theater* on TV every Saturday. They started at noon and played two Kung Fu movies back to back.

On the weekends my cousin was down, we'd watch those movies and go out and practice in the backyard. It was hilarious. We'd stuff pillows under our shirts and wear two layers of socks for padding.

Though I never pursued that interest or took lessons, I've always had a fascination with martial arts in general. I recently started doing my own kicking routine after looking up different martial arts workout videos.

Here's a typical kicking routine I do:

- Front straight kicks: 2-3 sets x 7-10 kicks
- Front snap kicks: 2-3 sets x 7-10 kicks
- Sidekicks: 2-3 sets x 7-10 kicks
- Modified roundhouse kicks: 2-3 sets x 7-10 kicks

Now, I'm no expert in martial arts and I don't plan to be in any type of fighting competition. I'm more inclined to give someone a hug than kick them in the face, but I do love the practice and plan to continue this type of training and discipline. I may even start lessons at some point. There's a spiritual and meditative side to martial arts as well, which I find interesting.

Another form of exercise that I absolutely love is kayaking and canoeing. I prefer kayaking out in open water. Of course, living in sunny Florida makes kayaking available almost year-round.

What makes kayaking challenging, especially in open water, is at some point you'll be paddling against the wind. For some strange reason, you feel like you're always paddling against the wind when you're in open water with no current. But it's loads of fun. If you've never gone kayaking, I suggest taking a lesson (or watch some YouTube videos) and try it out. Going down rivers can be fun as well. You're going with the current but there is paddling involved, and rivers can have obstacles that you have to maneuver around. Try kayaking or canoeing once or twice a month. It's a nice change of pace for exercise.

Our favorite place to kayak is called Weedon Island in St. Petersburg, Florida. It's a beautiful preserve with a mix of open water kayaking and going through these canals with mangroves. The mangroves have thousands of tiny black crabs. It's like you're in a horror movie, so your heart rate is up a bit.

Playing sports is another form of exercise, and depending on the sport, it can be intense. There are many who play team sports such as soccer, flag football, basketball, or softball. Along with the games comes practice, so there's a given two times a week workout. One-on-one sports such as tennis or racquetball can serve (no pun intended) as a high intensity workout.

You may be, or probably know a few people who are involved in the extreme races like Tough Mudder, Spartan Race, Warrior Dash, and several others. These are events with various obstacles you must conquer throughout the race. Obviously, something like this isn't a one-time event. This requires consistent training to get conditioned leading up to the event. In other words, you can't just walk onto one of these races out of shape and expect to finish. I've yet to do one of these, but I more than likely will at some point.

I could go on talking about the many forms of exercise that exist. Again, I strongly encourage strength training, or some type of resistance training, at least three times a week. The leaner muscle you have, the more efficient your body will function. You don't have to be or aspire to be a bodybuilder or powerlifter to have weightlifting as a part of your life. So, don't let that hold you back.

The point to all of this is simple: stay active. As much as I love sitting in the recliner watching Netflix, our bodies were not meant to be stagnant. Unless you're working a manual labor job, many of us sit for most of the day. We're just not built to do that. Heck, I'm sitting now while I'm writing this. I need to get up and stretch!

I want to encourage you to do something active each day even if it's just a fifteen-minute workout at home. You can do some push-ups, dips, and practice a little Yoga. Don't use the "I don't have time" excuse. If it means getting up a little earlier, do it. Go in the living room, pull up a quick workout video on YouTube and "get after it", famous line from Jocko Willink, decorated retired Navy Seal, and one tough dude!

Okay, so I spent a bit of time on workout information, and provided you with two types of workout programs that you can follow. I suggest you get started! Right meow!

"I'm sorry, did you just say meow?" - Super Troopers

Parting Thoughts, Gold Nuggets, and Extreme Focus

'Always remember, your focus determines your reality.'

- George Lucas

Parting thoughts...I almost typed "farting thoughts" instead! I've always had a deep appreciation for potty humor. Anyway, so we've covered a lot of ground. Even if you're not into heavy metal music (you really should be), you should still walk away with a few gold nuggets. At least I hope so.

I found my passions at a young age. However, I don't think that I fully dedicated myself to them during my early adulthood, you know, the years when you can really shape the direction of your life. I've heard several world-class performers and successful people talk about extreme focus. I didn't learn the art of that until later in life. The people that choose to be extremely focused on their goals are the ones that *make it* so to speak.

This whole rhetoric of multi-tasking is a complete lie and and a mere myth. I see this in many companies and workplaces, especially the corporate world. They want you to do more with less yet still expect everything to be right and go smoothly. It's a setup for utter failure.

Grant it, there are certain tasks that can be performed simultaneously without losing effectiveness. For example, I study Thai language while walking on the treadmill. I call this my *Learn and Burn* sessions. It's like practicing your vocal scales while driving. That's feasible and it makes sense.

However, if I were checking my emails and social media while attempting to write this book, I would more than likely never finish the book. The excuses would naturally flow: "didn't have time", "something came up*",* blah blah blah. If I were recording an album and trying to fit in chores around the house (Ugh, I absolutely dislike chores!), that would completely disrupt the process. I would either never finish the album or it would take seven times longer to put out. Even worse, it would have a ton of mistakes and missing pieces.

When you need to focus on a task that's of extreme importance, you need extreme focus. Our society tells us that we have so much to do, and that *to-do* list will continuously pile up to where it clutters your life. If that happens, you will indeed never have time for your passions and the things that you know you should be in pursuit of. You really have to un-clutter your life and either eliminate things that aren't important or delegate them. I adopted this philosophy after reading *The Four-Hour Work Week* by Tim Ferris.

I've learned over recent years to slow down and just breath. This is why I find ascetic disciplines such as Yoga and Tai Chi so valuable. They teach you to shut everything off and focus on the moment. It's a mental cleansing. Lifting weights has the same effect. When I'm in the gym, I'm not thinking about anything else other than the set I'm on or about to do. The gym is another example of the epic failure of multi-tasking. If you're sitting there playing on your iPhone, texting or whatever, you're not working out, and you're hogging the machine from someone that wants to work out!

Take a step back. Stop everything, and just breath. Start by taking in three deep breaths. You may think I sound like a monk (monks are cool) but this works wonders both physically and mentally, and I should add spiritually if that's important to you. Yoga is defined by connection to a higher power, or spiritual force, which results in the process of letting go. The Bible verse from Philippians 4:6 ties in quite nicely with that as well: "Be anxious about nothing."

The challenge is to spend some time analyzing your *to-do* list. Go through each item and ask yourself what would happen if this didn't get done. I have recently made a personal goal to eliminate as many tasks as possible and focus more on the items that have the most impact.

Think of it as building a big chest and having the choice between bench press or flyes. If you could only do one, bench press clearly wins because it's far more valuable to building muscle than flyes. I'm not saying ditch flyes. The analogy is based on if you had limited time for a chest workout and could only do one. You can build a big, strong chest with bench press. You're not going to reach that goal if all you did was flyes.

Another note on lifting weights: **you better focus 100% on what you're doing in the gym**.

If you're off in *la-la land*, as I was when I got clobbered in football practice when I was a kid, or if you're worried about work or something else, you're more prone to injury. Focus on the weights now. You can deal with the other junk later.

A huge part of having extreme focus is eliminating distractions. I think cell phones may be the greatest of these. TV is another big one. We can also be sidetracked by our thoughts. We must train our minds and send those thoughts away as quickly as they come in.

If you're learning guitar (or anything), dedicate a specific time each day or every other day to practice. During this time, shut everything else off. That means lock yourself in a room, don't bring your cell phone, and don't turn on the computer. There should be no interruption unless someone is dying. In all seriousness, schedule realistic blocks of time to focus on the task, and stick to it. This is how you go from good to great, from mediocrity to excellence.

The Final Countdown

'The kingdom's ours and growing stronger.'

- Tom Englund, Evergrey 'Archaic Rage'

We've dug pretty deep here in a variety of areas, and some of this book brushes along the lines of self-help. So, I want to end on a lighter note (although I prefer heavy notes, aka metal!). And there's no better way to do that than to have a chapter named after a cool Europe song.

As each phase of life, and each day for that matter, has its own sets of challenges, we have to learn to enjoy every moment we're alive. How is this done? Pursue your passion, or *passions*. There's nothing greater than being knee-deep in the things you love the most, the things that you feel you were put on this earth to do.

Once you dive in head first, you'll discover so many little pathways that have the potential to lead to something cool. I'll give you an example. I always dreamed of being in a rock or metal band when I was younger, touring the world and all. Despite the reasons that didn't happen, which I take full ownership of, I didn't throw in the towel. I later found other avenues that allowed me to continue my musical endeavor.

Here I am, three albums and one single release deep, and now writing a book based on two of those albums. Let that be an encouragement to you. When you're consistent, you force opportunities upon yourself. They may have a twist and may not align perfectly with what you had envisioned, but that's okay. Chances are, that newfound path may work out better than what you initially had in mind.

You must stay on your path in pursuit of your dreams, but at the same time, you have to be open to the many possibilities that may come along as a result of your quest. Let it be a journey, because, "someday love will find you."' Okay, that was a deliberate Journey pun.

Create a vision for your life and focus on that. Don't let anything stand in the way. Yet at the same time, don't take yourself too seriously. Have fun with it.

Love life. Love yourself. Love other people too. Love what you do. If you're working out, embrace the weights. There will be some pain, but it's a pain you'll start to welcome. If you already lift, you know what I'm talking about.

If you're a musician, recognize that you have a gift. Spend as much time with your instrument as you possibly can. If it's your voice, sing often. If you are an actor or aspiring to be one, chase that dream and go to as many auditions as you possibly can. You can apply this approach to anything in life. Practice, commit, and dedicate yourself. Get good, get even better, and become the master of your own version of what you're doing.

In the guitar world, we call this a "signature sound". You can tell it's Slash on the guitar from the very first note that's played. The same goes for Joe Satriani, Steve Jai, Kirk Hammett, and so forth. You become one with what you put your heart and soul into, and you end up creating your own genre, something that no one can ever replicate.

I've thoroughly enjoyed this specific journey (writing this book). It's like we're sitting down over coffee, or perhaps a nice craft beer, and just having a chat. And it's been quite a pleasure. As I always say, keep it metal!

Printed in Great Britain
by Amazon

16842033R00072